WHERE
DO YOU GO
TO GIVE UP?

BUILDING A COMMUNITY OF **GRACE**

WHERE
DO YOU GO
TO GIVE UP?

BUILDING A COMMUNITY OF **GRACE**

C. Welton Gaddy

Smyth & Helwys Publishing, Inc.
Macon, Georgia

ISBN 1-57312-005-7

Where Do You Go to Give Up?
Building a Community of Grace

by C. Welton Gaddy

Copyright © 1993
Smyth & Helwys Publishing, Inc.
6316 Peake Road
Macon, Georgia 31210-3960
1-800-747-3016

Library of Congress Cataloging-in-Publication Data

Gaddy, C. Welton.
    Where do you go to give up? : building a community of grace / C.
Welton Gaddy.
    xiv+167pp.   6 x9" (15 x 23 cm.)
    Includes bibliographical references.
    ISBN 1-57312-005-7
    1. Grace (theology) 2. Spiritual life—Christianity. 3. Gaddy, C.
Welton. I. Title.
BT761.2.G344 1993
234—dc20   93-34372
                                                          CIP

Contents

To
The Faculty, Administration, and Staff
of
The Southern Baptist Theological Seminary
1963–1970
(a wonderful fellowship of learning
in which faith was strengthened,
growth was encouraged, and
community was discovered)

Preface

You need to read this book. Please do not think my judgment presumptuous. You really do need to wrestle with the material in this volume. For at least two good reasons.

First, you need grace. Not a doctrine of grace. Not an ideology of grace. But the reality of grace. You need to experience grace. Everybody does.

Awareness of a need for grace varies from individual to individual. Some folks straight-forwardly confess their longing for grace. Others repress even a recognition, to say nothing of an acknowledgement, of their need for grace. Still others have no clue that life holds any possibility for an experience so superlatively wonderful as an encounter with grace. Of course, then, they have no awareness of a need for grace. But, it's there in everybody. Recognized or not, confessed or not, a need for grace exists in all people.

A successful search for grace requires knowing what grace is and where grace can be found. Such knowledge seems simple enough to acquire. But, rarely does it come as easily as you might think. People looking for grace discover cruel imposters and experience bitter disappointments. For some reason, many of the individuals who talk most about grace demonstrate little comprehension of the biblical meaning of grace. And they live gracelessly. Not uncommonly, hurting persons desperately desirous of finding grace reach a point of despair, seriously questioning the reality of grace.

An ability to identify the traits of a community of grace can prevent needless hurt. Reaching out for grace inevitably involves personal vulnerability. No reason exists to risk an abuse of such openness like that which predictably occurs when individuals seek grace amid fellowships where grace does not exist. Pain, rejection, and disappointment are minimized when a quest for grace probes relationships that bear evidence of the presence of grace. Finding an authentic community of grace helps every bit as much as encountering counterfeit fellowships of grace hurt.

You need the real thing. Genuine grace. You need to experience an authentic community of grace. This book is about fleshed-out grace.

Second, you can be a medium of grace: a source of blessing, even salvation, for scores of people around you who are searching for grace. Or, if not searching for grace, just trying to find a way to get away from life as they know it. Uncountable numbers of folks have given up—given up on themselves and on life. They are ready to run away. But most do not know where to go. Even if they have thought of a community of grace, the idea seems more fanciful than real. They feel trapped. You can make a difference for good among such people. You can help build the kind of community to which they can turn, a fellowship in which grace exists as an indisputable reality. This book contains suggestions for the construction of such a community. You need to read this book. Honestly, that is not just a sales pitch. It is a general observation about any individual seeking to be a whole person. And up to this point in my life, that observation has never been challenged by a single exception.

I needed to write this book. That is a personal confession.

Passion has pervaded my involvement in this project from start to finish—a passion to describe the need for grace, a passion to understand the nature of biblically defined grace, a passion to specify the characteristics of a life of grace, and a passion to encourage the formation of communities of grace. At stake in this work is an examination of issues crucial to the basic substance of my faith.

Is grace a fantasy or a reality? I wanted to know. Indeed, I felt I had to know. Pursuing an honest answer to that inquiry compelled me to try to distinguish between what is biblical and what is cultural, what is essential and what is superficial, and what is true and what is false regarding grace. A frightening question formed the foundation for my investigation, "Does Christianity work or does it not?" What began as an academic inquiry quickly developed into a spiritual pilgrimage—a journey of belief.

Two authors in particular challenged my inherited, and until recently unexamined, beliefs about grace. Robert Farrar Capon, an Episcopal minister, disturbed me with his relentless advocacy for unconditional grace. In book after book, Capon commends radical ("hilarious") grace with an exquisitely crafted, theologically-oriented logic informed by insights gained from his meticulous exegesis of pertinent biblical texts.

You can't judge a book by its cover. Never was this cliché more true than as a description of the best selling novels of Andrew M. Greeley. This prolific author-priest conveys profound theological insights in reality-based fictional narratives that he calls "parables of grace" (or sometimes "comedies of grace"). A long time ago I turned to Greeley's stories for entertainment. Repeatedly I have found in them enlightenment.

I thought I understood grace. But a time came when I was no longer sure; Capon and Greeley prodded me to re-examine my views on grace by way of a serious study of the scriptures. As a symbol of my gratitude for the delightfully helpful aggravation of these two authors, brief quotations from a few selections of their published works appear at the beginning of the major sections of this book.

The more I read and learned about grace, the weaker I found my previous conception of it. My desire to look at grace afresh became stronger and stronger. Then a blitzkrieg of difficulties hit. Bombarded by problems (some of my own and many belonging to others), I watched persons critically in need of grace stunned, and often floored, by people who treated them with no trace of sensitivity and an apparent abhorrence for grace. The desperation of that situation formed the "final straw." I found myself filled with the passion that catapulted me into this project and sustained me as I worked on it.

I have written what follows with enthusiasm, anger, sorrow, excitement, disappointment, and hurt. Not one word has been put in print passively or matter-of-factly.

Dealing with the biblical literature was problematic. Long-standing prejudices and presuppositions got in the way. I had to set aside previous assumptions about what the Bible says and replace them with convictions formed by what I was discovering the Bible actually says about grace. At times the magnitude of the chasm separating biblical commendations of grace and ecclesiastical expressions of grace has overwhelmed me.

Frequently I have battled troublesome confusion trying to understand why many of those who delight most in parading righteousness defiantly deny grace to those whom they consider unrighteous when, according to the scriptures, grace is the basic component of righteousness. Repeatedly disappointments prompted doubts regarding the viability of the gospel in church or society. I kept trying to decide if grace is fact or fiction.

Affirming God's grace presents no real problems for me. But, discovering God's grace mediated through people is another matter altogether. I continue to fight a cynical conclusion that the grace that abounds in God is nowhere to be found even among those who claim an identity as God's people. However, my hopes have been buoyed by the Bible's numerous promises about grace. And, I have been encouraged by the discovery of a few fellowships of men and women committed to living out the Bible's truth about grace.

Appreciation abounds for numerous persons who have trusted me with their gut-level feelings about grace. All the people and situations I have written about are real. In a few cases, I have altered circumstances and individuals' names to protect the privacy of the persons involved.

Judy, John Paul, and James—my wife and our sons—constitute the community of grace that I know best and the primary fellowship within which my work on this book has been done. Though personal experience must be examined in light of biblical teachings in a pursuit of truth, these three people have provided me with excellent fleshed-out examples of scriptural expectations. Not always understanding my preoccupation with and passion for this project, I am sure, Judy, John Paul, and James have nevertheless supported an extended period of time devoted to my writing.

I am impatient. Hurting people abound. So does God's grace. Why is it so terribly difficult to get the two together?

Why do so many people who speak about grace so eloquently relate to people in trouble so gracelessly? It is time, using the language of an old cliché, to call their bluff, "Put up or shut up."

Is a community of grace possible? Is grace a fundamental truth or a highly-touted falsehood? Is grace fact or fiction? Is grace an elusive fantasy or an available reality?

I have an opinion about the correct answers to those questions. Unless I have masterfully deceived myself, this opinion is informed by divine revelation—in the Bible and in Jesus Christ. I will make no effort to hide my recently-come-by convictions about grace in order to stage a dramatic declaration of them at the book's conclusion.

God's grace cannot be confined to a one-time experience of conversion. All of salvation is about grace. What is received from God is to be shared with people in need. People who really experience grace live gracefully in relation to everyone. The grace-laced identity of God's people finds its clearest expression in the consistency of a grace-based ministry extended to all persons.

Grace is real. A community of grace is possible. God's architectural design for this development awaits the work of a construction crew made up of people like you. I offer this book with hopes that it will help get that grace-work underway.

C. Welton Gaddy

Acknowledgements

Authentic grace has a face. Or faces. What I have written about grace on the pages that follow derives from interaction with specific people as well as from reflection on biblical theology.

Floyd and Ann Craig are longtime cohorts in mercy. In recent years, they have turned their house into the "No Agenda Retreat Center" and welcomed scores of hurting people to come there, live with them, be quiet, rest, and heal.

Joe Paul and Emily Pruett readily share the grace they claim. Devoid of fanfare or flair, these two friends exercise mercy as enthusiastically as they enjoy life.

Elmer West, Guy Sayles, Jim Strickland, and Howard Bramlette use the telephone literally to "reach out and touch" people with their affirming acceptance and multi-faceted assistance.

Eleanor Nutt has a "sixth sense" regarding friends' times of need. She follows her instincts with helpful personal contacts.

Individuals like Julian Cave, Bob Moon, Kenneth Powers, John Smith, and Jane and Wesley Turton extend grace and re-enforce hope without talking much about what they are doing.

Ernest Campbell conveys substantive grace through brief hand-done notes as well as by way of his nationally-acclaimed pulpit ministry.

Rodney and Wanda Collins and David and Debbie Bailey make weekly Saturday-morning breakfasts occasions for spiritual encouragement with soul-lifting, side-splitting laughter.

John and Sunny Lane know that relational support is not without difficulty. Each can engage in the kind of conversation that transforms a dinner of enchiladas, rice, and refried beans into a sacramental meal.

Walter (Buddy) and Kay Shurden wade right into both problems and pleasures with their friends. Unintimidated by surrounding circumstances, Buddy and Kay stand with those they love, embracing them (literally) and laughing or crying together as family.

Floyd Thatcher encouraged my interest in this project from the very beginning and as I wrote offered helpful suggestions regarding its direction.

Harold Twiss provided expert editorial counsel that allowed me more effectively to get in print what I felt throbbing in my heart.

Individually, these people comprise indisputable evidence of the viability of grace. Together, they exist as incarnational arguments for the possibility of a community of grace. Apart from relationships with these folks, I doubt that I would even believe in grace much less be able to commend it.

I.
Run for Your Life

"Christianity starts by telling you that you have no place left to go because you're already home free; and no favor to earn because God sees you in his beloved Son and thinks you're the greatest thing since sliced bread. All you have to do is explore the crazy Mystery of your acceptance."

Robert Farrar Capon
Hunting the Divine Fox

"The peculiar thing, Father . . . I can't explain it at all is that my grief was joy. I was sobbing with joy. Pain and ecstasy all mixed up, grief and gladness confused, so I couldn't sort anything out. What do you call that, Father Lar?"

"Grace, Maria."

Andrew M. Greeley
The Cardinal Virtues

"Sometime I want to go to the airport, catch a plane, and fly away. The destination doesn't matter. I will not tell anyone I am leaving. I don't know about coming back. (A pause.) Someday, I may do it. (A longer pause.) But, I probably won't."

A long-time friend was speaking. Honesty always has been a given between us. Never before, however, had I heard these words from him. Tom spoke his first sentences about leaving with optimism, even tempered excitement. His resolution conveyed a spirit of profound longing. Only Tom's concluding words reflected sadness. Pessimism about doing what he wanted to do, he later explained, had nothing to do with an absence of desire to act, only a realistic assessment of his lack of courage. Obviously, my friend was troubled and hurting.

Tom is not alone in his situation. His sentiments are far from unique. In our society, troubled people abound.

Sara has cancer. She just found out. Though she needs time to sort through her feelings about what is happening, she gives attention first to her husband and children. Something inside Sara tells her she must be strong. But that is very difficult. A crippling weariness develops as Sara tries to cope with her anger, fear, and anxiety while voicing an optimism that she does not feel and faking an energy that is not within her. Sara receives counsel as comforting as a stoning: "Sara, honey, you know we just can't understand life. God's ways are not our ways. Maybe there is a purpose in all of this that we cannot yet see. I do hope you will continue to smile and be strong. You are such an inspiration to so many of us." Sara wants to scream or run or both. Must people always have advice? Will no one embrace her if she is honest? Is there not anywhere Sara can let down completely, vent her irrational anger with a curse, shout her questions to the heavens, confess her fears and sadness, and cry with no inhibitions?

Steve and Pam are having an affair. Yes, both know better. It all started simply; they would say, "innocently". Pam works in Steve's office—a very competent employee who, because of her job, probably understands Steve's professional concerns better than anyone else. The pressure was on. Year end reports were due soon and major company goals had not yet been met. Steve was worried. That made Pam worry.

One evening after work, the two colleagues met for a cup of coffee—neither can remember who made the suggestion. Rapport was immediate. Each could talk to the other about concerns that seemed to be of no interest to the people in their homes. Fireworks went off in their imaginations. Professional conversations gave way to expressions of personal intimacy.

Ask either Steve or Pam how things are going and you will hear talk of "the best relationship in the world." But, both are afraid. A public disclosure of their relationship would ruin everything that each of them always has felt important. Cautious attempts have been made to get advice. In conversations begun in search of help, however, even their veiled references to "someone else," a romantic interest, pushed the "start" button on a machine programmed to play clichés on subjects falling under the rubrics of admonitions, judgments, and threats—cliches that Steve and Pam cannot bear to hear even if they need to hear.

Can no one understand their situation? Will no one accept them where they are regardless of concerns for where they need to be? Must honesty from Steve and Pam inevitably lead to terrible consequences? Each wants to run (sometimes to the other, sometimes with the other, sometimes from the other). And, in time, each, in one way or another, will run.

Joan and James are frantic about their teenage daughter. Typical rebellion has escalated into terrorist revolution. Sonja, the daughter, has moved beyond hurtful words to disruptive, anti-social behavior, endangering herself and others. Feeling guilty and angry, the parents are immobilized and bewildered. "What did we do wrong? Maybe we didn't spend quite enough time with her earlier. But we went the whole route with the PTA, scouts, and the city soccer league. Why? Why is this happening?"

Now Sonja has disappeared. Joan and James want the police to know, but no one else. The same words come from each mouth: "I can't stand the embarrassment and humiliation of this becoming public information. You know how people will look at us and judge us to be bad parents. What horrible things will they say about our daughter? I just want to run and hide forever."

Is there a place to which Joan and James can run and be comforted? And, what about Sonja? Is there a community in which Sonja can sense immediately that she is understood by people more interested in helping her than condemning her?

1.
Everybody Hurts

Everybody hurts—in some way or another; if not now, earlier or later. Troubled people abound in our society.

Invariably that assertion is met with arguments to the contrary. Names are called and families are described as exceptions to the observation. How little we know of what we think we know!

I spend a great deal of time listening to people talk about each other. A woman speaks of an acquaintance her age: "She sure has life all together. I would love to be like her." Two men refer to a business associate: "He never has a problem." A couple in therapy comment on two people recently wed: "That marriage has everything going for it. Those two have got it made." A worried grandmother speaks of her neighbors with a sigh, "Oh, what I wouldn't give to be a part of a family like that." I listen and in each instance I think, "If you only knew what you are saying."

The young woman who exudes security wears a mask of confidence to hide an inner terror fed by conflicting values, dissatisfaction with relationships, and a fear of the future. The businessman with a problem-free appearance borders on panic because of a recent realization that he is locked into a profession that is like a prison for him. But, he would go to any extreme to prevent anyone from seeing him as less than optimistic. The supposed model couple married out of duty not love. Both the husband and the wife are resolved to live a lie until such a life is no longer bearable. The envied family presents a picture of happiness and care in public. But in private, relationships are being ruined by jealousy, competitiveness, and resentment. The parents are devastated.

How can people be so mistaken about each other? The problem is not merely one of perception. Society tends to instill within persons a strong capacity for denial accompanied by remarkable abilities in dramatic deception.

Individuals like Tom, Sara, Steve, Pam, Joan, James, and Sonja live in every neighborhood. They can be seen working in their yards, playing with children, walking their pets. As much as anyone else, these people attend public worship services, reading the litanies, singing the hymns, and generally looking respectably spiritual. Even a sustained study of these people reveals no problems. All appears well. When these individuals speak to each other or to someone else and the traditional "How are you?" is asked, every one of them responds, "Just fine."

Self-introspection at this point can be very revealing and aid understanding. How often do you say what you really think or feel? Do most of your actions show your true intentions? Or, do you tend to feign happiness even when hurting and speak lightly, even if feeling burdened with the weight of the world?

Culture has done a number on us. The socialization process that defines acceptable behavior and spells out basic priorities produces virtuoso actors and actresses, masters of deceit. People who have done their homework well can respond to a friendly "How are you?" with a quick, convincing, "Great," "Terrific," or "Wonderful," despite the fact that their emotions are in disarray and their stomachs knotted by anxieties. We even like for corpses laid out in caskets to look as alive as possible.

Granted, at times the ability to rise above pain and not voice complaints is a healthy dimension of maturity. But as a way of life, it is a different matter. When troubled people consistently attempt to appear untroubled, more trouble, more serious trouble, is ahead. Duplicity, "putting up a front," or intentional schizophrenia—call it what you will— exacts a heavy toll.

Why do we do it? Why is deception about hurts preferred over honest confessions and requests for help? Repeatedly people offer one answer to these questions.

2.
A Basic Assumption: No Grace

The world is without grace. That assumption provides the motivation for our cover-ups of negative emotions. It is the foundation of our deception about weaknesses, mistakes, and failures.

Self-protection is a real concern. "We must look out for ourselves. People not only will write us off relationally if they discover we are plagued by problems, they will talk about us unmercifully"—so the reasoning goes.

Strange, but true. Study groups are for the smart. Welfare services often by-pass persons too old, too weak, and too uneducated to request them. Business opportunities are available primarily to those who succeed. Churches cater to saints rather than sinners. Potential employers, associates, or clients are turned off by dosiers that document job terminations and health reports that record hospitalizations. Much like financial institutions' preference for loaning money only to people who have money, social relationships tend to shower love most lavishly on people already surrounded by love.

In this odd situation, many pleas for help go unrecognized. They are subtle, if not silent, and masterfully camouflaged. Not wanting to appear weak and unacceptable, problems-laden persons slip into a critical condition before anyone notices their difficulty. Hyper-panic sets in. Or deep depression. Irrational behavior erupts. Danger accompanies every decision and action.

Grace takes on problems. Grace refuses to shy away from difficulties. Grace initiates actions to do good for a person or persons, deserved or not, requested or not.

To live by grace is to accept people where they are (even if they seem unacceptable), to love them as they are (even if their actions are unlovable), and to work for their good (even if wringing their necks is more desirable). Graceful people are helpful people. Though accomplishments, strengths, and joys are causes for celebration, where grace prevails, failures, weaknesses, and sorrows are not reasons for rejection.

"That ain't the way it is!" The words are spit out like poison darts by a young woman whose every attempt to turn life around has been met by someone pushing her back or putting her down. A similar reaction to the promises of grace comes from individuals whose marriages have failed, whose politics have become unpopular, whose characters have been assassinated by newspaper stories (true or false), whose finances have run short, whose ethics have been questioned (not determined, only questioned). Negative!

A reality check reveals a society intrigued by success, threatened by loss, and intolerant of mistakes. Though no sane person within an organization actually professes perfection, expectations of near perfection are an integral part of the insanity that characterizes a corporate mindset. There, little, if any, room is available for losers. Individuals in need of help are pitiable but expendable distractions within social structures, excess commodities clogging the economic corridors that lead to bigger and better accomplishments. Dismissal is deemed best for those who have suffered defeat. After all, public institutions cannot afford to be sensitive and caring toward private individuals. Such an idyllic attitude would slow down intolerably the mechanized-like thoughts of leaders in industry and grind to a despicable halt the "movers and shakers" of society.

Often an organization's "official line" to troubled people nods at sensitivity. But, actions tell the real story. Far too many times a gesture of understanding is extended toward a person just prior to dismissing her and pressing on.

A personnel officer carefully measures her words to a recent applicant for an open position: "We like to give people a second chance. Frankly, however, we had one bad reference on you. Though the negative comments of concern were not corroborated by anyone else and we suspect an ulterior motive behind them, we cannot risk it. We do wish you well as you continue to seek employment."

The chairman of the board stoically speaks to the CEO of the company: "You really have done a good job for us. Most of your work is exemplary. But some of the executive committee members have heard rumors about how you spend your weekends. They are a bit uncomfortable. Personally, I don't believe there is a problem. However, I want your resignation."

A member of the nominating committee in a local church pietistically shares his opinion about a potential elected leader of the congregation, "I like the man. If the decision were mine alone, I would recommend him for the ballot. You know, though, we have to protect our reputation as a congregation. Like it or not, the institution must be given precedence over an individual. We can't be elevating to church leadership positions people who have made moral errors."

Evidence of a world without grace is convincing, at times well-nigh overwhelming. It's not difficult to understand why multitudes of people fearing rejection mask disappointments, cover up mistakes, and fake indefatigable optimism. No wonder so many people are hurting.

A community of grace is needed. Virtually no one argues that point, not even those who judge it to be a wild pipe dream. Some folks scoff at all talk of a grace community, however, branding it as radical idealism or the hallucination of other-worldly religionists. They admit, "It would be great if it were possible." Then rush to exclaim, "But!" (a way of indicating) "I don't want to hear any more about it."

Resentful of skeptics' negativism, though appreciative of their recognition of such a fellowship's worth, other people expend their energies to make a grace community a reality. They see a merciful fellowship as both a logical outgrowth of authentic humanism and a promise at the heart of the Christian mission.

Despite unanimity regarding the need for a community of grace, work towards its establishment often gets delayed by discussions of merit. Trying to decide what people deserve sidetracks efforts to give people what they need. Misers of grace want to be certain that recipients of their good gifts qualify as worthwhile persons. So, the very individuals most in need of grace face the slimmest chance of ever receiving grace.

Who or what is to blame when people are troubled? Attempting an answer to that question requires an audacious attitude and a god-like vision. Yet, assigning guilt and specifying a person's "just desserts" is a popular hobby. Few fear it at all.

Anytime a married couple has serious trouble, acquaintances press to discover who is to blame. Individuals out of step with their friends are scrupulously inspected to determine if they should be charged with an offense. A son leaves home in a fit of anger. Some neighbors castigate his parents for insensitivity. Others point a finger at the boy and bemoan his uncontrollable temper.

Most assessments of people's behavior tend to overlook mixed motives and unintended developments. If a situation is bad, no good can exist in it or come from it. That's that! If a person is truly good, she will not be a part of anything bad. No ifs, ands, or buts about it. Thus, the centuries-old, divinely-inspired teachings of Job go unheeded once more. Falsehoods prevail. An attentive look can distinguish the good guys from the bad guys every time. All questions have easy answers. The "Dragnet" detectives of conventional piety declare, "Just state the facts. Who was right and who was wrong? Who are the victims and who are the victimizers?" Simplicity is demanded. Complexity is disregarded.

A preoccupation with merit is not the only hindrance to graceful help for people who hurt. Advocates of a "let the chips fall where they will" mentality argue that people should be allowed to get what they deserve. So, amid problems caused by mistakes or sins, a measure of mercy goes to the innocent (though the real purists shake their heads and comment that people ought not allow themselves to get in situations where problems can arise and questions be asked). And, as for the guilty—God help them! Because no one in a kangaroo tribunal of moral justice will help them.

Judgment is a waste of time for persons motivated by grace. Understanding the source of troubles and assessing blame to the appropriate individuals are not virtuous activities. What is crucial is what, if anything, is being done to help the troubled people.

While a community group waits to distribute food until the causes of wide-spread hunger in their area can be determined, people die of starvation. Whose fault is it? The bad politics of a local official. The greed of merchants. The selfishness of the powerful, *or* the merciless people who would not share food with anyone until the blame for hunger could be placed on someone?

Two teenagers face the prospects of a child born to them outside of marriage. Their requests for help are met by relentless inquisitions: "Who started this relationship? Who requested sex? Why didn't one of you think of contraception? What are you going to do about your sin? Who will accept the primary responsibility for this wrong?" While the push to press charges against one of the teens continues, both run—either seeking to find a way to make a home together for their child, ready or not, or seeking entrance into an abortion clinic. Who is at fault here—the boy, the girl, their parents, *or* the judicious individuals so interested in identifying a scapegoat that grace is ignored? (Maybe the answer is all of these or none of these.)

Troubled people seldom, if ever, find help in rational explanations of their situations. Most know how they got where they are. But, knowing is not the issue. Hearing accusations of guilt while hurting is of no benefit. Needed most is mercy. Unconditional expressions of compassion are in order. No substitutes for grace exist. If only troubled people could turn to a community of grace!

Well, what are the possibilities? Honestly. Is the assumption of a world without grace beyond challenge? All who dare to answer such questions had best be sure that when they speak of grace they are talking about the real thing.

Grace is not to be confused with kindness or equated with being nice. Operative grace is much more than an exceptional response to a critical situation. Grace goes far beyond the realm of a religious belief alone. Grace is a way of life.

Grace embraces risk and creates within its practitioners a vulnerability to hurt. Grace refuses to be deterred by strong words against it and hostile reactions to it. Grace expects to be suspect. The dirt that must be touched to care for individuals mired up in it does not offend grace. Bad reputations fail to frighten grace. Possibilities of being judged harshly for not exercising judgment cautiously cause no worries for proponents of grace. People committed to grace know their best efforts may be (probably will be) condemned as immoral placations of evil.

Grace is up front. Grace is for every day, not just special days; for every situation, not merely occasional ones.

Communities of grace are possible. But multiple difficulties make their formation tough. Building a community of grace requires unwavering intentions, stubborn compassion, hard-headed determination, and exacting, energy-depleting work.

Correcting the common assumption of a world devoid of grace requires herculean efforts. A good place to begin is with a recognition of the secret troubles that plague people's lives, accompanied by an appreciation for the hurting's tendency to hide their pains and an understanding of their desire to run.

3.
Troublesome Situations and the Temptation to Run

Given people's tendency to hide their problems and the necessity of recognizing hurt as a prelude to offering help, here is a checklist of trouble-producing, crisis-creating phenomena. Anytime these realities are present, a strong possibility exists that the people involved are troubled. They well may be disturbed to the point of an eagerness to bolt and run.

Individuals trying to cope with critical developments that require major adjustments in their lives need help: grace. Persons interested in providing a community of grace have to be sensitive to and informed about these problem-filled experiences of transition.

Personal

An individual not at peace with herself is unlikely to find much satisfaction in any aspect of her daily activities. Yet, she pushes the very concerns that are most troubling to her into deep hiding.

A severe lack of *self-esteem* creates havoc in a person's existence (at any age). A lack of confidence, a sense of unworthiness, a feeling of ineptness, an inferiority complex—any one of these or all of these—stunt personal growth, block social involvements, warp emotional expressions, and prevent productivity. Correction develops as a result of acceptance, affirmation, and encouragement in the individual's life. But, signals are mixed.

On the one hand, a person is taught the reality of self worth. Teenagers are urged to take care of themselves. Self-assertiveness is prized. Then, along comes a band of cynics, often disguised as "honest realists." Personhood is devalued by these people. They understand an individual to be of little more significance than a number—a file in a government records office, a cog in the gears of industry, a weapon in war, a potential consumer for marketing specialists, a matriculant for educators.

Re-enforcement of this negative assessment of personhood comes by way of both culture and religion. Fast-paced business associates race toward their next success completely oblivious to the individual concerns of anyone, even a friend. Fire-breathing spiritualists equate self-interest with selfishness. Demeaning the self is considered a sign of faith.

Worthwhile or not? What is a person to believe? The mixed messages create confusion about an individual's value. Any sense of self worth is jeopardized. And, if uncorrected, that mentality rapidly erodes self confidence. Finally, a person concludes: "I am nobody!" Following close behind that declaration is the suspicion "There is no place for me here." Then comes the temptation (or an outright intention) to run.

Persons who normally possess a healthy self-concept can lose it. Prolonged *disappointment* and incessant *stress* contribute to this loss. A vicious cycle cripples people. First, hampered by disappointments and strained by pressures, reasoning abilities are weakened, emotions are damaged, and judgment is impaired. Bad decisions follow. Then, questionable actions take place. Next, even if external criticism is not immediately forthcoming, internal, self-induced rebukes develop. Disappointment deepens. Stress intensifies. A driving desire to give up finally dominates all other concerns.

Physical illnesses and *emotional illness* precipitate crises. Unfortunately, an activist society demonstrates little sympathy for persons who are sick. Work must continue. The organization must prosper. No program can be allowed to suffer.

Persons with physical disorders fare much better than those with emotional problems. Victims of heart attacks, lung disease, or blood-related difficulties eventually are re-integrated into normal professional and social processes, though caution and suspicion about them are obvious. Persons who must contend with anxiety attacks, paranoia, and depression have no such guarantee. Derogatory remarks about people who see "shrinks" are standard fare for them.

Remember the trauma of a United States senator quickly removed as the national Democratic Party's candidate for the vice-president of the United States upon the discovery that earlier in his life he battled an emotional illness. More recently, a revelation that he had taken a new anti-depressant drug turned into a near fatal charge against a popular candidate for a congressional seat in a state election.

Understandably, many people who are ill and know it fear telling the truth about their condition and asking for help. Not only are these individuals troubled about being sick, they are troubled about other people's reactions to their illnesses.

Personal difficulties not properly addressed tend to worsen. Often such unresolved problems lead to *chemical addiction, institutional dependency,* and/or *abusive behavior,* each a form of "running." Whatever the specifics, the situation is a tragedy. And, at the very time the affected people need understanding, acceptance, and compassion more than ever, they are less likely than ever to receive from their peers what really will help them.

Familial

Homes house hurt as well as happiness. In family relationships, joy can exceed all imaginable limits. But so can pain. Sadly, many persons attempt to confine family-related difficulties (or, to hide them) within the rooms of their residences.

Trapped! The feeling is a prevalent one. Two people, who in their younger years confused exciting sexual experiences together with enduring compatibility, realize they do not belong together. Each is a source of severe dissatisfaction for the other. But, from their families, from their church, and from their colleagues at work, they receive relentless pressures to stay together. Sensing hemmed in and not understood, each burns with an anger that is not likely to be dissipated apart from some form of destructive behavior.

An only child cannot ignore her responsibility for a *dependent parent*, who needs constant assistance but fears a nursing home worse than death. The young woman loves her elderly father and wants to help him, but feels desperate to get on with her own life. Repeatedly she forfeits her interests in new relationships, career opportunities, and social organizations for the purpose of offering support for her dad. Eventually, rage sets in. She senses that life is totally unfair. Then, terrible guilt develops. At moments, this despairing daughter fears that she is being smothered. No one is available to help. She feels trapped, miserably trapped.

Betrayal broadsides a couple about to celebrate their tenth wedding anniversary. The wife confesses involvement in an extra-marital relationship. The stunned husband reacts with predictable panic and anger. His pride is wounded. Embarrassment about the situation spreads through the whole family. A competent therapist helps the wounded couple interpret what has happened and examine the factors that contributed to it. He holds out not only a promise of the continuation of the marriage but the possibility of a strengthened relationship by means of long-term therapy. But, neither partner can decide whether forgiveness and a re-establishment of trust, honesty, and intimacy are desirable even if possible.

A mother and father scream about *disobedience,* indecency, delin-quency, irresponsibility, and immorality when they discover that their college-student son has moved into an apartment with a young co-ed he has dated for two years. Amid their verbal assault on his decision, the son picks up indications that his parents are much more concerned about their place in the community, their reputations, and their embarrassment than about his welfare. Denouncements and threats virtually destroy all avenues for parents-son communication and the interaction that will be so important in the future.

Divorce is as stigmatic as it is prevalent. Hyper-critical judgments and stereotypical labels burden persons involved in divorces regardless of the specifics of their situations. Whatever relief divorce provides in one area of their lives is tempered by the problems that divorce creates in other areas. The adjustments that a divorce necessitates economically, socially, and relationally often look more like insurmountable problems than temporary transitions.

Frequently, the *death* of a family member sets in motion a series of destructive developments. In addition to legitimate *threats to security,* all of life seems altered negatively by the striking absence.

Not uncommon in all of these family situations are variations of *unfocused anger, unresolved grief,* and *needless guilt.* Apart from thera-peutic attention, these phenomena can contribute to major *clinical depression* and even an inability to function.

Much has been written about *runaway* youth. But, escape as a solution to family difficulties knows no age delimitations among its prac-titioners. Runaways from home include parents and children, wives and husbands. Most can identify what they are running from. Few can identify what they are running to.

Social

Masks hide the troubled spirits of innumerable people in all segments of society. *Deception* exists as a capstone virtue in the socialization process. Thus, individuals whose lives are ravaged internally don the looks, assume the postures, and conform to the images popularly perceived as signs of social success.

A woman, feeling the weight of the universe on her shoulders, speaks to a conference as if she is on top of the world. She is noted for an exemplary positivism, the envy of other CEO's in the city. Allowing others even a glimpse of her true feelings is too big a risk. She must fake strength even if she doesn't have it.

A teenage girl becomes fed up with playing the games, faking the attitudes, and simulating the enthusiasm necessary for a successful pursuit of popularity. Her sense of personal integrity is under siege. But, she doggedly continues her performance. Right now, being popular seems more important than being honest.

A much-admired man in the business community daily denies his dreams and ignores his values. If he resigns his prestigious position to do the menial missions work to which he feels magnetically drawn, no one will understand. Both the goodwill of his peers and a salary from his company will be lost. And, likely he will be labeled an irresponsible kook.

Perception is not reality, despite the constant hype of image-makers and symbols-sellers. Pleasant words and a smile on the face cannot compensate for depressed thoughts or eradicate a hurting heart. Playing a role that contradicts one's true identity means taking up residence in the stifling environment of a shrinking room with no exit. While the public may be impressed by an individual's deception, the person of deceit senses the death of all that is important in life. Often such a person concludes, "I cannot live like this any longer; I must either find some place to which I can get away and go there or die."

Not all refuge-seekers in society enjoy the luxury of privacy in dealing with their troubles. A headline in a morning newspaper announces an IRS investigation of the president of a local bank. Whether guilty or innocent of any wrong doing, the elderly gentleman immediately is made the subject of hushed conversations and harsh suspicion. An evening newscast raises a serious question about administrative policies in the public school system. Though no specific charges are leveled against anyone, everyone in the administration becomes fair game for negative speculation. A grand jury's decision to question a popular civic leader is quickly made a matter of public information. Most people assume this woman must be guilty of some wrong or she would not be summoned into that judicial setting.

Rumors kill people as effectively as an overdose of drugs or a blast from a shotgun. Persons have been ostracized, families discredited, and careers terminated by irresponsible talk. Few listeners bother to raise questions about the sources of incriminating information about other people or the motivations of those persons eager to "tell all" about someone. Distinctions between fact and fiction receive little attention. Conventional wisdom incorrectly concludes that "where there is so much smoke, there is bound to be some fire."

Full-scale *scandals* are not uncommon. Critics hurl labels at the individuals involved like darts aimed at a bull's eye marked *indiscreet, immoral,* or *illegal.* Getting close counts almost as much as a direct hit on the target. Once a person is even remotely associated with one of these bad words, the nasty work of reputation devastation is underway. The criminal justice system's verdicts regarding illegality can look like penalties handed out in a playschool compared to the judgmentally-motivated, mean-spirited antics of retaliation inflicted upon "the guilty" by individuals and institutions intolerant of even questionable, much less evil, behavior.

I know well several people who refuse to attend public functions or even engage in conversations with acquaintances. They sense that adversaries constantly watch, judge, and condemn them. Perhaps silently. For sure wrongly. No bars are needed to keep such folks confined in their self-constructed prisons.

Professional

"Business is business, you know." The phrase is almost magical. Speak these words and an interest in persons can be subsumed under profits, public relations concerns, management structures, and benefits for the bureaucracy on a list of important corporate priorities. Everybody understands that is the way things are in the world of business. Ironically, in the very arena in which people's troubles proliferate, virtually no provision is made to aid troubled people. Hard-nosed executives employ macho terminology to state the standard rationale for this situation: "It's a dog eat dog world." "This is no place for patsies." "If you can't stand the heat, get out of the kitchen."

"The authorities" view *bad judgments* and *mistakes* as mortal sins. Business types cannot afford to be soft in their response to such developments. The fact that a woman's error in her projection of monthly sales receipts resulted from fatigue induced by all-night care for her hospitalized mother cannot be taken into account. "After all, we all have problems." A similar judgment arises in response to a bad decision by a unit leader preoccupied with, if not depressed by, his wife's announcement that she wants a divorce.

Errors are deplorable and failure is intolerable where success has been assigned a near god-like status. All employees are expendable. Progress by the organization is the preeminent concern.

Termination from a salaried position can devastate a person. Inestimable damage is done to the dismissed individual internally—loss of self-respect, besieged by insecurity, overwhelmed with embarrassment, and embittered about the future. Additionally, hasty and uncritical public opinions about the person make the rounds. Almost irrelevant are questions such as: "Was it best for the person?" "Did this action represent the triumph of a principle over a position?" "How was justice done?" Harmful assumptions prevail: "Obviously she did something very wrong." "He cannot be counted on." "That person might as well forget any kind of meaningful employment."

Amid a preoccupation with doing—assessments of identity based upon activity, and determinations of personal worth by the figures on a pay check—*unemployment* is the professional equivalent of AIDS. Remuneratively-rewarded working people tend to remain at an arm's length distance from their unpaid peers. After all, something must be bad wrong with individuals who do not have a job. Devoid of tasks that command a salary, many people succumb to serious trauma. Their sad plight is sustained by other people's insensitive reactions to them as well as by their own sick opinions of themselves.

Conversely, innumerable people would like to get out of their jobs. However, they either do not know how to make a change or do not want to deal with the consequences of leaving their current positions. Faced by a pervasive "onward and upward" mentality, individuals find little understanding of or support for their desire to "cut back" or "step down." Tragically, many folks who cannot consciously make the decision to vacate a position subconsciously find a way out. Often their method of escape is questionable at best and irresponsible at worst. Then, a whole new set of troubles emerges.

Of course, colleagues speak of their desire to help professionally troubled associates. No doubt, with good intentions. But in reality few folks take time to offer the kind of assistance needed by problem-plagued people. Everybody gives attention to their own jobs. After all, you know what they say, "Business is business."

Spiritual

Spiritually troubled people are often the most difficult to identify. They fool themselves as well as others, confusing living by faith with avoiding a recognition of problems.

A major malady can be paraded as intense spirituality. Examples abound. *Obsessive selfishness* disguises itself as a remarkable *humility* in order to provoke praise (which is respectably dismissed outwardly—"Oh, I don't deserve those compliments"—and tightly grasped inwardly—"Yes!"). Displaying *spiritual strength* akin to Samson's physical might covers up serious *emotional insecurity.* Relentless activism in support of good causes attempts to relieve an *unhealthy sense of guilt* and to satisfy an insatiable need for forgiving acceptance. *Rank prejudices* pass as *admirable convictions. Narrow mindedness* poses as *doctrinal certainty. Irresponsibility* in relation to others hides behind a portrayal of absolute *dependency on God. Escapism* from the world dresses up like a *pre-occupation with heaven.* Sadly, righteousness and sickness become almost indistinguishable.

Pervasive misunderstandings of God, faith, redemption, and the church are the molds that determine the shape of major troubles for many people. Religion is transformed from a freedom to be enjoyed into a burden to be carried. *Self-denial* in service to Christ is misinterpreted to mean *self abuse* as the will of God. Imagining that God's goodness is dependent upon human goodness, individuals burn out in their *pursuit of perfection.*

Wrong-headed thinking that makes humanity synonymous with sin causes people's attempts to achieve the impossible goal of becoming more religious by being less human. Surmising that whatever is normal must be immoral, people seek a way of life that is as unrealistic as it is irreligious. Serving God is seen as a form of life-narrowing bondage rather than as a gift of life-enhancing liberation. Thus, the depths of faith are falsely measured by degrees of misery.

All the troubles stated here theoretically can be seen incarnationally. I know each one of them by name. By a multitude of names actually.

A minister sends his daughter away from her family because she is *pregnant* and *unmarried.* He cannot afford to have his "influence" adversely affected.

A woman who has been involved in an *extra-marital love affair* assumes she is devalued as a person forever. Convinced that she is beyond God's forgiveness and useless to the church, she wants to run away. Peers re-enforce her despair.

A congregation shamefully castigates a wrong-doing member. Church leaders posit that exercising *judgment* is more God-like than expressing compassion.

Teenagers grappling with predictable *doubts* remove themselves from all church organizations. They feel that their questions about belief and confessions of disbelief make them unacceptable among people of faith.

A young woman who has had an *abortion* finds it difficult to live with herself. Moreover she is unable to relate to others. Unrelieved guilt dogs her every step. Religionists decrying abortion as a sin beyond redemption relegate this woman to a mind set that is life threatening. She buys it. She's had it with them, with God (as falsely represented), and with herself.

Preoccupied with an act of repulsive sin in his life, a man deems it more religious to wallow in remorseful guilt than to be set free by God's forgiveness. His words are telling: "I don't deserve forgiveness. I don't merit happiness." The man needs to hear someone say, "Well, of course not. Who does? Forgiveness is God's decision, not ours." But he sits slumped over, shrouded in silence.

Sick religion quickens a person's desire to run, to run away. When people's troubles are associated with their faith and enmeshed in fellowships of faith, however, they may develop a desperation-inducing conviction that they have no place to which to run. Sadly, then, in search of helpful relief, individuals turn their backs on the very communities that can serve as places of refuge, dispensaries of God's grace.

4.
In Praise of Exits

Several years ago, in one of the major urban centers of the northeastern United States, a bus driver and his bus disappeared. A later explanation of what happened provoked an interesting display of public reaction.

For years, this bus driver had guided his over-sized vehicle down the same streets of the city and made the same stops at the same places at approximately the same times to pick up many of the same passengers. One day, weary of a routine that had induced boredom, the driver decided he had had enough of it all. That morning, he steered his bus out of the company parking lot and embarked upon his route, but he made no stops. He just kept driving. He drove through the city, out of the city, and away from the city. When the proper authorities finally found the man and the bus, both were in Florida.

When this bus driver was brought to trial to be prosecuted for his criminal behavior, an avalanche of protest letters overwhelmed officials of the court. Writers pleaded for leniency and the release of this man, explaining that they knew the same kind of boredom that had motivated his decision. Many indicated a strong desire for the courage to take some action similar to that taken by the bus driver.

If the attitude of that bus driver was once latent and seldom expressed in public, that is no longer the case. Presently the sentiment behind his action enjoys a broad-based popular acceptance and widespread enthusiastic affirmation. Indeed, a new breed of hero and heroine is being applauded.

Jonathan Coleman's factual account of the story of Jay Carsey in *Exit The Rainmaker* attracted a great deal of attention and generated wide spread discussions.[1] Carsey was a respected college president. One day, after careful, secretive planning, he walked away from everything and everybody he knew. To the absolute astonishment and alarm of the college, the community, his friends, and his family, Jay Carsey just disappeared. Seeking refuge—without any vision or definition of its nature—the forty-seven-years old executive ran (actually he went to the airport, boarded a plane, and flew away).

Remarks from Carsey's friends provide telling evidence of the pervasiveness of a normally unspoken point of view. When Jay's sister was informed of her brother's surprise exit from a normal life with no forwarding address, the caller said, "Susie, that boy is crazy. He's lost his mind." The sister responded, "No, he's found it."[2] One of Carsey's business colleagues, a "figure of responsibility" in the local community, spoke for many who remained silent, "If only Jay had chartered a plane, we all could have gone."[3]

Almost everyone is capable of making such a mad dash for an exit. Carsey acted on an idea that innumerable people harbor in their minds but never dare talk about or make plans to implement. No one, particular type of person or profession possesses a monopoly on the aspiration to run.

Viewers of the popular movie "Shirley Valentine" find in the character for whom the film is named a heroine somewhat akin to Jay Carsey. Unlike the former college president (because of his advanced education, academic position, and social station), though, Shirley Valentine represents great numbers of the populous. She is not the leader of anything. Her life is like most lives—working at a job to make money to pay monthly bills, working at home to perform the responsibilities dictated by her stereotypical role as a rather submissive wife, occasionally finding her spirits lifted by her dreams, but more normally bending under the weight of unfulfilling routines.

To the surprise of almost everyone, including herself, one day, with exceptional boldness, Shirley Valentine embarks upon a holiday to Greece. What she intends as a sight-seeing trip becomes a life-changing journey. She experiences a joy she had seldom, if ever, known in Manchester, England, feeling almost reborn. When the time comes for her to return to her home, she is deeply, sadly disturbed. Her will is torn. She rethinks the unparalleled happiness of her recent days, anticipates a painful re-entry into the deadening familiarity of daily routines in the past, and speculates about who will miss her if she fails to return home.

Not until Shirley arrives at the airport departure gate in Greece, the passage way through which she is to board a plane back to England, is the matter resolved in her mind. Just before handing the airline official her ticket, in a split second, she makes a decision that alters her life forever. She turns away from all she has known and gives herself to an uncharted venture. Shirley Valentine's comment about that dramatic moment establishes her as the heroine of scores of people who dream of possessing the boldness to follow in her footsteps: "I'm not running from life, I'm finding life."

The growing popularity of such movies and books (of which these two are only representative) reveals the pervasiveness of the reality they capture. Jay Carsey and Shirley Valentine are the envied images of innumerable people like Marion, Sarah, Joan, James, Steve, and Pam, whose situations were described at the beginning of this section of the book, and of my long-time friend Tom who still harbors thoughts of someday catching a plane and flying away forever.

Difficulties pervade the best of lives. Pursuing happiness at all costs becomes a most unhappy enterprise. A desire to run, a longing to escape, and a gnawing need to find a refuge are common ingredients in the human condition. Not at all exceptional.

When an individual struggles with stress, strains to get rid of troubles, and/or feels trapped, the possibility of getting away takes on the dynamics of an urgent necessity. A will-to-escape mentality cries out for attention. And action.

Troubled people abound. The need for a refuge is profound.

Is a refuge available? Is a community of grace possible? Where *do* you go, where *can* you go, to give up?

II.
Where Do You Go to Give Up?

"I was an occasion of sin for him," she snapped. "How could I have been an occasion of grace too?"

Andrew Greeley
An Occasion of Sin

"God has no problem with losers. . . . God in Christ has bigger fish to fry than preventing sinners from sinning. His paramount purpose is to drag the whole world into the party; if you make good behavior any condition at all, you blow the Good News of his purpose out of the water."

Robert Farrar Capon
Health, Money, and Love . . .
And Why We Don't Enjoy Them

Charlie Brown charges a football, tenuously held upright against the turf by his friend Lucy. Obviously the little fellow is eager to get his foot into the pigskin and send it soaring. In a split second, though, determination becomes exasperation. Just before Charlie's foot touches the ball, Lucy jerks the sphere from his path. It's a joke; nothing new in the relationship between these two. Lucy tricks Charlie again.

But Charlie is not quick to quit. Whatever frustration and aggravation he feels are outweighed by trust—trust in Lucy. With resilient hope, Charlie allows a repetition of the same scene. Again and again he runs toward the ball to boot it skyward only to have Lucy play the same prank on him every time. Finally, Charlie has enough. With desperation detailed on his uniquely-rounded face, Charlie turns away and asks, "Where do you go to give up?"

This classic pictorial sequence from the artistic genius of Charles Schultz is my wife's all-time favorite cartoon. She is not alone in her choice. Millions of people have viewed this particular "Peanuts" episode and smiled quietly or maybe even chuckled aloud.

Cartoons allow us to laugh about matters that ordinarily would spark anger, provoke anxiety, or make us cry. That is one of their values. Charlie Brown's question prompts a humorous response as long as it remains on his fictitious lips, made-up words in a make-believe dialogue. But if Charlie's words surface in our minds or spill across our lips amid a crisis, the impact of the question is much different.

Face muscles twitch. A lump clogs the throat. Stomach pains signal wads of nerves threatening to wrench one's entire body into a knot. Periodic shudders of anxiety race up and down the spine. Finally a question (*the* question) emerges, silently or audibly: "Where do you go to give up?"

A haggard sales person wearies of racing from one airport to another. Increasing numbers of contacts to be made obliterate possibilities of rest. And, the job is devoid of security.

A lack of social acceptance discourages a former drug addict. Job opportunities are nil. Initiative dissipates along with self-respect.

A young housewife despairs. An endless barrage of infant-related chores that must be repeated with nauseating monotony douse her dreams of the glories of motherhood. A nagging tug at her spirit threatens long-standing commitments.

Trauma grips an elderly individual. Adjustments imposed by an undesired retirement quickly erase the joys of a golden wedding anniversary celebration. Then the beloved spouse dies.

A middle-aged man loses his job. After numerous unsuccessful attempts to secure employment, he loses his desire to work. Gone also is any sense of self worth.

Individual outcries comprise a chorus raising questions about a giving up place. Does such a place exist? Is there a giving up place?

"Where *do* you go to give up?"

What is needed? What is a giving up place? Obviously, it is a place of healing. But, that is too general. What are the specific qualities of such a place?

In a giving up place, understanding is prevalent and questioning is absent. Acceptance does not have to be earned and behavior defended. Weaknesses do not have to be masked for criticisms to be avoided. The reason for a person's presence in this place is far less significant than responsiveness to that individual's needs. What happened yesterday is not nearly so important as what is happening today and what can happen tomorrow. Protection from more hurt is promised as a part of a devotion to help. Sitting and crying are as much in order as running and laughing. Brokenness is recognized as a credential for service. It is OK not to be OK. Forgiveness is extended even before it is requested. Redemption is every resident's agenda, their only one.

Only a community of grace qualifies as a giving up place. Substitutes do not work.

One of my friends attempts to avoid working through personal difficulties by spending money. When her problems mount, she heads for the shopping malls. But, the relief does not last. End-of-the-month bills inflated by compulsive buying sprees to "get away from it all" remind her that nothing has actually changed except the figures printed on that darkened line labeled "minimum payment due."

Other problem-plagued acquaintances buy a ticket to a movie and seek to lose themselves in someone else's world. No sooner have the credits at the end of the film begun to roll, however, than these people's difficulties rush back to the front of their consciousness.

Sadly, some folks seek to go somewhere else without ever moving physically. But their crises are only worsened by the use of mind-altering drugs or an over-consumption of alcohol.

Sometimes geographical movement away from a troubling context provides temporary relief for disturbed people. A brief change of scenery may prove beneficial—a trip to the beach or a hike up a mountain trail. Removing one's self from normal responsibilities and stressful relationships for a while can help—an extended sight-seeing vacation or a prolonged stay in a retreat center. A period of hospitalization may even be required. Seldom, if ever, though, does a change in geography actually alter a difficulty. Problems have a way of packing up and traveling with us. At the very least, they trail us from a distance for a while and then suddenly show up for a surprise visit.

In dealing with difficulties, retreat, escape, and procrastination are sometimes far more wise than irresponsible. Perhaps the right moment for a confrontation with haunting problems and efforts aimed at their solutions has not arrived. In such situations, sojourners have to stay on course despite insensitively-hurled charges that they are fearful of reality, charges that highlight the pilgrim's need for a supportive community. No amount of mobility, however, can supplant the benefit of a loving, healing community. Even periods of relative privacy and inactivity for purposes of professional therapy need to be followed by personal involvement in a caring fellowship.

A community of grace—a giving-up place, a place to rest, a place to bask in love, a place to get well—has nothing to do with an escape from reality. By no means! At stake is a reality of a different order. Present here is a reality readily distinguishable from that commonly experienced in society, but none the less authentic.

Surely it is not shameful idealism or pitiable naivete to assume that within a given community an openness to failures is as "real" as a welcome for the successful. Are there not people as willing to embrace hurting individuals as to dance with happy ones? Protection from punishment can be as "real" as a compulsion to extract payment in full for every wrong deed a person has done. Reality can consist of the provision of a second chance as well as of a decision to write off all who have blown it.

Of course, the realities of a community of grace are far less familiar than what usually is labeled "reality." But truth is not defined by results from a popularity poll. Even a wide-spread lack of familiarity with a certain kind of community does not negate the authenticity of that community. A giving-up place can exist. A community of grace is a possibility.

The need for a refuge is not new. Neither are attempts to provide places of refuge. References to both the word and the concept of refuge are prominent in scripture and culture, in mythological religions and Judeo-Christian history.

5.
Cities of Refuge

Early Judaism prized the city of refuge as an important institution. The name came from Moses, the patriarch. Six such levitical cities were prescribed by the author of Numbers 35:6, 13-14, who instructed the appropriate people to construct three asylums on each side of the Jordan. (A listing of these six cities is available in Joshua 20:7-8.) With the passing of time, Moses called for the establishment of additional cities of refuge (Num 4:41-43).

Actually, barbarians and civilized people alike recognized an individual's right of asylum. At their holy shrines and in their sacred precincts, the Phoenicians, Syrians, Greeks, and Romans extended absolute security to all fugitives. No restrictions prevented an offer of hospitality to all persons regardless of their relationship to the law— innocent or guilty. Frequently, criminals, runaway slaves, debtors, and political fugitives resided in those refuges that prohibited revenge. Justice was not an issue.

Israelites made the provision of asylum more conditional. They welcomed into their cities of refuge primarily persons who had been involved in an accidental homicide, a crime of passion, or a murder without premeditation. (Some scholars argue that even murderers were admitted and assured an experience of justice.) Levites governed the cities of refuge with a will to prevent impetuous judgments and hasty vindictiveness. Residents were provided a place to live and protected from all avengers.[4]

Obviously the sanctuary granted by the cities of refuge in ancient Israel, as described in the Old Testament, fell far short of the mercy provided by Christ and his followers in the communities of faith described in the New Testament. But Israel was moving in the right direction.[5] The goal of the cities of refuge and any punishment associated with their existence was the restitution of fugitives, reclaiming wrongdoers for good (Josh 20:6). In these sites, grace tempered justice, even if ever so slightly.

Cities of refuge did not encourage irresponsible, interminable escape. They provided havens of immediate protection, provisions for crisis situations. Each community, replaced criticism with care and elevated encouragement to a position of dominance over judgment. Justice was not circumvented so much as transcended.

Negative consequences still accompanied evil. Sin caused suffering. There was (is) no way around those realities for anyone. But God's people sought not to add to anyone's difficulties. They extended to persons in trouble what God had provided for them. Cities of refuge promised comfort and consolation.

What a terrific breakthrough in ancient thought! What a wonderful idea to be studied! What a remarkable institution to be emulated! Here was a subtle hint of grace, a quiet whisper in Israel that would become an unmistakable shout in Christ. A refuge was a provision among God's people in the past. A ministry of grace is a non-negotiable staple in the compassion and mission of God's people in the present.

Where can a troubled person find even minimal mercy today? Currently, where can people on the run go to give up within a context of understanding and protection? Do the ancient cities of refuge have any contemporary counter parts?

6.
Communities of Refuge

Early Polynesian religious mythologies produced several refuge-oriented cities. In the first years of the fifteenth century, Pu'uhonua o Honaunau (place of refuge of Honaunau) was established as a sacred spot available to people in need of a sanctuary. This site on the Kona Coast of the big island of Hawaii has been preserved as a park.

Every phase of life for the Hawaiian people was directed meticulously by the *kapu*—literally translated as "restriction" or "forbidden" though generally understood as the religious law. Overestimating the importance of the *kapu* within that culture would be difficult. Yet, a community of refuge provided sanctuary even for people who broke the highly-respected religious law. Violators of sacred taboos were allowed to remain in the community of refuge until they were purified by the priests who resided there. When the lawbreakers departed, the protection granted by the community and the absolution bestowed by the priests remained with them.

One morning, I visited the grounds of the ancient Honaunau community. I sat in shaded grass listening to a descendant of the priests who had once served there. I walked along the shore line watching the turquoise waters of the Pacific wash against the bay where the ancient temple had stood. I stared into the rigid, actually angry-looking, carved-out faces of the gods that had ruled this region. All the while, I wondered how nearly five hundred years ago these primitive people latched on to such a grand concept as mercy and determined to institutionalize the practice of a remarkable form of grace. Also in my mind were questions about where, if anywhere, that kind of grace is guaranteed today.

Why have places of refuge not emerged among much more enlightened people? As I made my way out of this one-time sanctuary, I thought of all the people presently in need of such a place. I wondered if anyone would be interested in forming a community dedicated to making grace a reality once again.

7.
Houses of Refuge

Through the decades of the nineteenth century, the reefs, summer hurricanes, and winter storms along the east coast of Florida destroyed thousands of ships and claimed the lives of many of their crew members. The United States Life-Saving Service, an early predecessor to the United States Coast Guard, initiated a proposal to establish nine houses of refuge in response to that grim reality. In the late 1900s, the United States Treasury Department authorized funding for the construction of these simple structures (not to exceed a cost of $2,900 each).

One sunny, but blustery, spring day, I entered the only House of Refuge still standing. Gilbert's Bar is located on Hutchinson Island just across the waters from Stuart, Florida. Actually, seeing the dwelling was a bit of a disappointment—a simple wooden building with four sparsely-furnished rooms downstairs and an upstairs dormitory for twenty-four persons. Countless other houses much older in age are more attractive to the eyes. But, thinking about this house—the motivation behind its construction and the nature of its mission—that was something else, something very exciting.

The House of Refuge stood solely to serve people in trouble. Consider its location: a shore-line spot where storms were prevalent and danger was dominant. In 1875, the best possible site for the construction of this place of refuge was the worst possible site for taking up residence. Study its mission: the provision of a secure shelter for people with problems. The clientele of the House of Refuge were desperate individuals with multiple needs and few, if any, resources with which to express appreciation or to offer payment for their needs being met. Only as the supplies of the House of Refuge were being depleted in service to persons in dire conditions was its existence justified. Ponder its vision: not just to stand as a light house beckoning people to the stability of the shore, but actually to offer an always open sanctuary promising safety and security. Neither clock nor convenience dictated activities within this building. Storms and crises constituted the environments for which its work was intended. Needs set its agenda.

No restrictions barred an entrance to the House of Refuge for any one. Signs providing directions to the house were posted all along the coast. All seeking sanctuary were invited.

Through the years, a steady stream of sailors sought refuge for a variety of reasons. Questions and declarations about those reasons—Was the ship wreck unavoidable or the result of human error? What were you doing in this potentially dangerous area anyway? You did not think like a responsible navigator! Such foolishness as you exhibited deserves an onslaught of difficulty! Shipwreck serves you right!—did not matter. Everyone in trouble qualified for help. The reason for a need did not affect attempts to meet that need.

The House of Refuge was a permanent home only for the caretaker, the rescuer. For all others, it was a place of transition, a place to ride out the storm, a place of peace amid turbulent conditions, a place to find assistance, a place for fellowship with other persons battered and broken for various reasons, a place to rest, a place for wounds to heal, a place to get well. Though the length of people's stay there was not limited, a return to a productive life was assumed and encouraged. A constant turn-over of residents guaranteed that the space occupied by the weak who had grown strong could be made available to the next persons who showed up in weakness.

That windswept afternoon in South Florida, I stood on the porch and walked around the grounds of that rickety old building toying with the idea of this place as a model of a secular form of grace. Certainly the name was right—House of Refuge. What a service! What a powerful symbol! This structure merits consideration and emulation by people serious about practicing mercy.

But is anyone interested? Once again I pondered the existence, or lack of existence, of contemporary counterparts to such a sanctuary of grace.

8.
Groups of Refuge

In recent years, special-issue groups have proliferated in our society. Persons characterized by great diversity except for one common concern get together for understanding, encouragement, and counsel. The bases for these fellowships range from drug abuse to child abuse, a gambling compulsion to a lack of vocation, and infertility within a marriage to infidelity within a marriage. Alcoholics Anonymous, Single Parents Fellowship, and The Compassionate Friends are among the best known of these groups.

These fellowships work redemptively. Regular participants in them find sympathetic ears to listen to their confessions, therapeutic relief from their hurts, and invaluable resources for help. Scores of people have found fellowships of the self-help genre to be very useful as well as enjoyable.

After observing a support group convened by bereaved parents, a journalist for *The New Yorker* sought to define "the mystery and the miracle" witnessed there. Interestingly, the writer labeled what happened as "a dynamic," a "grace."[6]

Certainly all such organizations deserve commendation and duplication. However, they are single-issue and self-help oriented. Not all hurting people meet the narrow criteria required for receiving membership in these groups and ministry from them. What about the individual who cannot define what is wrong with her? Or, the man to whom the term "self-help" sounds like a death verdict? What is available for countless numbers of people whose problem-plagued lives are as complex as they are diverse? Where do they go to give up?

9.
What about the Church?

What about the church? Is not the church supposed to be precisely the kind of community in which grace abounds? Yes. But what *is* may not be synonymous with what *should be.*

Definitions are decisive. What is the church?

If "church" means the facilities, campus, and congregation denoted by a sign that reads "St. Luke's Presbyterian Church," "First Baptist Church," or "Holy Trinity Episcopal Church," its identity as a grace community is in question. To be sure, biblical theology suggests such a congregational identity. Scriptural conceptions of the church and social expressions of the church, however, often vary from each other considerably.

A young girl jaded and scarred by hurt after hurt asserts, "I am made to feel more uncomfortable in church than anywhere else I go." A middle-aged man hounded by crises comments, "I cannot stand the condescending looks which I receive from members of that congregation." A seeker-of-truth unwilling to equate simplicity and authenticity confesses, "The people in my church do not know what to do with me, so they ignore me."

Whether or not the church, any church, should be like that or is like that is not the issue. For these particular people, their comments reflect reality, the church of their experience.

Some argue vehemently, "*Our* church is *not* that way. Any discomfort those people feel is just in their heads." Others aggressively take the offensive, "Of course, wrong-doers will not feel comfortable in our church. They should not feel acceptable in any church until they change their ways. We maintain the highest standards of morality. We do not want anyone thinking that we approve of wrong-doers." Personally, both of these reactions make me uncomfortable.

Facing reality is a necessity. Sociology more than theology may determine the nature of a fellowship that defines itself as a church by a name on a public marquee. Often, a synthesis of faith and culture develops at the sacred altar. Then, within the camaraderie of believers even as within the structures of society, a premium is placed on perfectionism, uninterrupted growth, and success. In such a community, evidences of a discomfort with weakness and an intolerance with failure are not surprising. Despite continued scripture lessons in corporate worship, the spirit and actions of the members of the church tend to emphasize what people need to be saved from rather than what is saving.

But, sociology is not the sole culprit. Theology also can be a problem. Scholars all along the liberal-conservative spectrum of doctrine evidence a surprising unity in their assessments of the church's difficulty with grace. Frequently, even if a church's theology of grace is sound, its efforts to apply grace to troublesome relationships and implement grace in controversial ministries leave much to be desired.

David Seamands demonstrates convincingly how grace can be affirmed as a doctrinal concept but never incorporated into behavior by performance-grounded Christians.[7] As a result, what does not matter at all in the ministry of Jesus matters too much in the lives of followers of Jesus. Conversely, the grace Christ extends unconditionally is handled tenuously by people who meet in his name and offered to others only with conditions.

The church appears afraid of grace. Judgment is preferred. Obviously, judgment is easier than grace. "No" always sounds louder and more powerful than "yes." Trying to understand someone takes time and energy. Condemnation is a snap compared to the demands of redemption. Consolation is a drain. Besides, many church members have shouldered the Atlas-like responsibility of preventing anybody from getting away with anything that looks like evil. They have taken upon themselves the chore of venting what they (mistakenly) believe to be the inevitable vitriolic wrath of God.

Robert Farrar Capon posits that the church brandishes about judgment so ruthlessly that grace, the first and most important thing Christianity is about, is the last thing people now think of when they think of Christianity.[8] How sad!

This is not the whole story about the church, though. Signage, what is on a billboard in front of a meeting site, is virtually irrelevant. The nature of the people seeking to be a church is what counts. Church can be a fellowship of persons committed to the Lordship of Christ, a body of believers seeking to be obedient to God's will. Not perfect people, but people who, with God's help, are trying to be redemptive. Compassionate people. In this instance, a community of grace is a real possibility.

The problem is that not every group that calls itself a church is committed to a ministry of mercy. But any fellowship that is really a church exists as a refuge where people's needs are met with grace.

10.
A Community of Grace

Precedents for a community of grace exist. Both ancient and modern. Models of communities committed to the healing of hurting persons can be found in both sacred and secular history.

But not all storms are at sea. Lives get wrecked like wind-damaged ships. Though no officially recognized *kapu* currently controls life, a violation of certain taboos, written and unwritten, continues to be met with denunciation and retribution. Sometimes, even destruction. Hasty, uninformed judgments send people scurrying in search of acceptance and understanding. Naive agents of bad actions taken for good reasons receive the same condemnatory treatment as calloused individuals whose actions are intended for evil purposes. Persons reeling as if hit by the bullets of a firing squad watch their reputations ruined by a barrage of rumors. They long for a place to go where rest can be realized for themselves and rumors resentfully rejected by other residents.

Scores of people desperately need a fellowship for affirmation and redemption. Where can they find refuge? What about communities of grace in the present?

A community of grace is commended and encouraged, ideologically and practically. Honestly though, is the possibility of such a fellowship sheer idealism, merely a product of wishful thinking?

I must admit that sometimes the whole grace business seems too good to be true—that God is sovereign mercy, that at the center of life is grace. That, by the way, is a telltale confession. What does it say about human expectations that an idea of something good, really good, good beyond our wildest dreams, is suspected as untrue?

Little wonder that we have such problems with the gospel. Frederick Buechner sees a situation in which the news has been so bad for so long that only a precious few folks hear the good news. In Buechner's words, "People are prepared for everything except for that beyond the darkness of their blindness there is great light."[9] The same can be said of people's penchant for punishment over promise, denouncement over encouragement, and judgment over grace. All too often, even in the church.

A community of grace is a possibility! This is the unmistakable promise of the gospel. The realization of this possibility, however, involves far more than a verbal endorsement of the gospel as a grand and glorious idea. Work, hard work comprised of compassionate, nurturing efforts is a necessity if a community of grace is to be a reality.

I offer the words that follow as reminders of humankind's need for God's kind of fellowship. Prods to action are aimed at persons, like myself, who have been hesitant to affirm grace in demonstrations as well as in orations. For those courageous souls already busy about the tasks of centering their lives on grace and building communities in which all people are invited to experience life at that center, I affirm, encourage, and admire you. My goal in writing is not to add to the growing amount of literature on grace to be read. Rather, I hope to inspire and to encourage serious attempts to incarnate grace within human gatherings, among people honestly devoted to scriptural truths and compassionately in touch with contemporary needs.

III.
Bottom Lines

"Grace, I have learned, lurks everywhere, even, perhaps especially, in disappointments and failures."

Andrew Greeley
Confessions of a Parish Priest

"The gospel of grace is the end of religion, the final posting of the CLOSED sign on the sweatshop of the human race's perpetual struggle to think well of itself."

Robert Farrar Capon
Between Noon and Three

Grace is what the gospel is about. From beginning to end. Jesus is the incarnation of grace. Individually, disciples of Jesus are agents of grace. Collectively, authentic fellowships of God's people are vibrant communities of grace.

Most people agree about the primacy of grace theoretically. Grace has been a recurring object of affirmation in Christian hymnody and liturgy. Grace is considered an important doctrine theologically. But, practically, grace is far from sovereign. Unquestioned as a venerable belief to be accepted, grace is suspicioned as a fundamental guide for decision-making. Grace is rejected as a basic principle to be implemented in daily living.

Actually, a lot of talk about grace makes some people exceedingly nervous—theologically fidgety and behaviorally uncomfortable. In the minds of many, a strong emphasis on grace apparently suggests a watering down of ethical expectations, a weakening of religious discipline, a cheapening of threats of judgment, and an attempt at avoiding the consequences of sin. "We must not allow our expressions of grace to cause anyone to question our strong opposition to sin!" is a consensus thought. Unfortunately, some folks seem to prefer the worst to the best, the gospel as bad news to the gospel as good news.

If grace is a belief with little consequence for behavior, what does that say about the gospel? Are the promises of the gospel merely the substance of wishful thinking rather than foundations for a way of living? Is the gospel out of touch with life—insensitive to realities and idealistic about possibilities?

Answers to those questions are absolutely crucial when studying the potential for actually forming a community of grace. A serious look at the nature of the gospel in the New Testament is essential.

The gospel knows both the best and the worst about life and how, by the power of God, the best can come from the worst. Good is not affirmed at the expense of sin being denied. To emphasize the redemption of persons by God is not to ignore persons' rebellion against God.

Within the New Testament, an emphasis on grace emerges despite a well-nigh cosmic effort to elevate law over grace. Then (as now) religionists exerted enormous pressure to put grace in its "proper" place—a lofty attribute of God; a component in personal behavior so negligible as to be almost irrelevant to human affairs.

Grace is not a subject for sacred precincts alone. It never has been. Debates about grace represent much more than a tempest in a theological teapot. Grace transcends the category of an academic proposition. Grace issues are issues of life and death. In the gospel, grace and its promise of life receive an exclamation point at the expense of the murder of Jesus of Nazareth. The gospel heralds good news not because of an absence of bad news but because of the pervasive presence of the sovereign, redeeming God who is grace.

The gospel addresses life so profoundly because the gospel is bound up with life so intimately. Here are three bottom line affirmations of the gospel. Each, a non-negotiable statement of truth, has importance for all who will give themselves to the construction of a community of grace.

11.
Reality of Sin

To emphasize grace is not to minimize sin. Anyone who argues to the contrary ignores the gospel of the New Testament. There good news and bad news intermingle. The reality of sin appears most clearly in the grace-laced ministry of Jesus. Frightening insights into the severity of sin and gory descriptions of the effects of sin stand right alongside wonderful declarations of the promises of grace.

What is sin? That question has only one answer. A proper response to it, however, may take several different forms and utilize a variety of terms. Sin is rebellion against God. Sin is a rejection of the divine will. Sin is ignoring God's revelation. Sin is disobeying God's guidance. But the offense of sin involves more than God alone (though never excludes God).

Sin is a person refusing to be who God created that person to be. Sin is stopping short of growing toward maturity. Sin is living as less than a holistic human being.

Predictably, society cannot be excluded from any insightful discussion about sin. Sin is failing to relate to other people as persons created in the image of God. Sin is ignoring the needs of individuals. Sin is a refusal to serve as a conduit of God's love. Sin is withholding grace from anyone.

Sin is all of that. (And more, actually. Sin is the abuse, destruction, or pollution of God's creation.) But no one definition excludes the others. To ignore the needs of persons is to disobey the Word of God. An act of rebellion against God represents an individual's decision to stop growing and to attempt living as a lesser person than she or he was created to be. Sin involves a person's relation to God (separation), to creation (abuse), to self (perversion), and to others (lovelessness).[10]

The consequences of sin are horrible, so terrible that they are almost incomprehensible ultimately, if not immediately. Admittedly, separation from God does not seem to be too big a deal as long as a thousand and one "things" are available to claim people's attention and to fill the various voids in their lives. But, try to imagine the meaning of eternal separation from God in an existence in which God is all that matters, in which a relationship with God is the only source of fulfillment, joy, and peace. Where that thought prompts a gasp followed by "Oh, Hell!"—in words or feelings people come close to getting the point.

Likewise, right now, not being all the person God intends one to be probably fails to appear as a condition of earthshaking importance (much less an issue of eternal consequence). "After all, who is?" people cynically ask. Innumerable ways can be found to cope with incompleteness. Convincing rationales for irresponsible immaturity know no end. The matter seems to be more psychological or biological than spiritual. But, again, activate the imagination. Envision a situation in which the best of life can never be known apart from holistic development. Take into account that the greatest happiness-inducing gifts possible are unavailable to persons who deliberately stop short of their divinely-appointed destinies. What if God cannot be experienced joyfully just because personal wholeness has been ignored and life approached in an irresponsible and selfish manner? If, when contemplating such developments, individuals find themselves thinking, "God help us!" truth is within their grasp.

Ignoring people's needs in the present is as simple as turning one's head away from unpleasant sights, not reading newspapers or watching television newscasts, or ignoring a church's calls to individual involvement in ministries. No regret, not even a second thought, about a refusal to ponder (much less respond to) a pressing need may occur. After all, there is always something else to do—a symphony concert to attend, a book to read, a Bible study class to join, a game to play. Neighbors need not be allowed to get in our way unless they can benefit us.

Contemplate the truth that an absence of acts of love in a person's life adversely affects (well nigh destroys) that person's spiritual well-being. More specifically, in a context in which a relationship with God is the only relationship that matters, the only factor of any significance at all, an individual hurts God (turns her back on God) by failing to see and to respond to the needs of another human being.

Images of the ravages of sin protrude from both the ancient scriptures and contemporary culture. Look at beaten-down, broken-spirited individuals for whom the only thing worse than the conflict-loaded situations in which they must function daily is the debilitating war that constantly rages within their souls. They embody personal devastation. Their names may be well known: Saul, the king of a mighty nation; Jack, the CEO of a multi-national corporation; Samson, a fallen public hero from the past; or Jeffrey, a scandalized political leader whose story is the front page text in this month's tabloids.

Sin wrecks relationships (wrenches them apart, ruthlessly rips covenants into fragments). Note the relational debris that surrounds numerous familiar characters: David, the beloved musician, whose family disintegrated into shambles; Abraham, the patriarch, whose desire for security prevailed over integrity and resulted in a betrayal of marital fidelity; Nan, a longtime Sunday School teacher whose husband and children speak her name with a bitterness that borders on hatred; and the Caldwell's, a blue-blood family racked by firestorm-like fights fed by insane jealousy among the brothers and sisters.

What sin can do to a nation is as apparent in the civil sovereignties of the present as in the social structures of ancient Judah or Israel. Documentation of the destruction requires a long list: chaos in the streets, injustice in courts of law, hunger among the poor, a passion for the production of weapons of violence, crime in business, scrambled social priorities, and widespread cynicism and distrust.

Sin costs dearly, commands a price expensive beyond measure. Anyone prone to decision-making by the principles of cost accounting can be overwhelmed by the inestimably high sales tag attached to sin.

Unmistakable in the crucifixion of Christ is the horrible reality of sin and its inextricably close relationship with grace. How could people starved for a relationship with God become murderers of the Incarnation of God? What does this mean?

The crucifixion of Jesus dramatically demonstrates the lengths to which people—even (maybe especially) good people—will go to deny the prominence of grace. At the same time, the cross of Christ convincingly declares the extent to which God will go to establish the unrivaled sovereignty of grace in all of life.

Jesus was crucified by his contemporaries because he embodied and commended the grace of the eternal God. Then (and now), the populous assigned many concerns a much greater value than grace—law, tradition, justice, and religion to cite a few. Jesus stood as a threat to proponents of each of these priorities because of his insistence on the preeminence of grace. Thus, even devotees of religion desired the destruction of Jesus.

People will stop at nothing to silence grace. Far more concerned with sin than with grace, even religious leaders refused to believe that anyone could live by grace in a world of sin. Jesus did it. But, most of his contemporaries wanted no part of it. So, the Son of God was murdered in the Name of God. The cross of Christ stands as a giant exclamation point on the horizon of the cosmos emphasizing humankind's negation of the viability of grace in this world.

God, not God's people, has the last word though. With divine power, God took the most despicable rejection of grace possible—the crucifixion of Jesus—and turned that event into an eternal affirmation of grace. From the worst came the best. God transforms the damnation of Jesus *by* people into an act of redemption *for* people through Jesus. At the very moment when individuals tried their hardest to relegate grace to a subordinate status in all schemes of values, God established the supremacy of grace forever.

"Were you there?" A beloved old spiritual raises that haunting question regarding everybody's participation in the cross event. Similar words of inquiry spill across the lips of Marcellus, the central character in Lloyd C. Douglas' classic *The Robe*. Maybe that is the concern of all people who seriously ponder the dynamics of this stark tragedy. Were you there? Was I there?

The answer is "Yes." Whisper it or shout it. But, by all means, admit it. In a sense—a real, non-fictional sense—everyone participated in the crucifixion of Jesus. Though the faces around the cross change from generation to generation, the crucial issues remain the same. What killed Jesus in the first century would kill Jesus in the twentieth or the twenty-first century. Sin is a reality. And, everybody is guilty.

From this perspective, looking at life from the place of Jesus' death, much prevalent talk about sin takes on the character of nonsense. Asking "What did you do wrong?" or "What is your sin?" is unimportant. What kind of casuistry of compassion do such inquiries imply? Do we think ourselves capable of accepting some sins as understandable and thus forgivable while categorizing others as more inexcusable and thus unpardonable?

Who dares rank the severity of sins? What difference do our distinctions between evils make? After participating in the killing of Christ—which we all did—what else matters? The scholar-evangelist from Tarsus was right—all have sinned.

Then, too, seeing sin from the soul-shaking vantage point of the cross makes passing judgments on other people's sins appear to be the ludicrous activity of a crazed mind. How can any person condemn the sin of someone else—whatever the nature of that sin—when both persons—indeed, all persons—are guilty of the crucifixion of Jesus?

Sin is a reality. Sooner rather than later we would recognize that fact experientially even if we did not confront it as a truth asserted biblically and a doctrine affirmed theologically—a bottom line of the gospel. But the reality of sin does not (cannot) negate the primacy of grace. Not in the gospel. Not in life. Again words from the apostle Paul strike home with an unalterable truth—where sin abounds, grace abounds more.

12.
Availability of Forgiveness

The possibility of divine forgiveness is a certainty. Every bit as much a certainty as incontrovertible acts of human sinfulness.

Evil deeds evidence disobedience to the divine will and affect a separation between their perpetrators and God. Look, though, at the divine response. God confronts sinners with a sadness born of compassion and the stringent efforts of a love aimed at granting forgiveness for and establishing reconciliation with the people involved. Just as no individual stands apart from the propensity to sin, no person exists devoid of the availability of forgiveness for sins. God has acted (and acts) in a manner beyond the comprehension of most people to secure this bottom line truth of the gospel.

The true nature of divine forgiveness has been distorted almost beyond recognition. Frequently, people attach legalism, presuppositions, and conditions to forgiveness. Peter (that is the disciple Peter prior to the crucifixion and resurrection of Jesus) could be the patron saint of such folks.

As much as Peter relished the promise of forgiveness from God, this fiery apostle had major problems with the idea of unlimited forgiveness in relation to his contemporaries. Peter wanted parameters within which to function, laws that would establish carefully delineated boundaries beyond which forgiveness was not necessary. So, he asked Jesus to specify the exact number of times forgiveness had to be offered before it could be discarded.

The reasoning behind the fisherman-disciple's question is as current as our most recent problem with a person. "Enough is enough," we say. If forgiveness can be taken for granted, some people will take advantage of it. Trying to do right will not even matter to them. We need a law—a stopping place—about forgiveness rather than an open-ended principle. Otherwise, our kindness will be abused."

Jesus rejected outright that kind of rationalization against unlimited forgiveness. The identity of the advocate for such thought—whether Simon Peter or one of us—does not matter. In his refusal to specify a point beyond which forgiveness cannot go, Jesus revealed the unconditional nature of God's grace.

Peter wanted to restrict the number of times forgiveness could be offered. Others sought (seek) to establish prerequisites for its realization:

In order for forgiveness to be extended, a particular place must be visited—the temple, a church building, the altar at the front of a public sanctuary. In order for forgiveness to be received, a certain attitude must be displayed—self-denigrating, emotionally opulent sorrow. Likewise, specific words must be spoken—"I have sinned. I am unworthy of redemption. I beg for forgiveness."

Conditional forgiveness is a human concoction, not the product of divine compassion. Jesus never made the possibility of forgiveness dependent upon a particular locality, mentality, or liturgy. Jesus forgave persons who needed to be forgiven. What do the words and actions of Jesus mean in contemporary controversial situations where forgiveness is made dependent upon certain conditions? Or, does the ministry of Jesus really matter?

"We would like to forgive William for his wrongdoing." A church group discusses a member who has been condemned by and estranged from the fellowship. "But he has not come to us confessing any wrongs, displaying any regrets, or asking for forgiveness. Thus, he has left us with no options. We cannot be of any help either to him or to his family at this point."

"I would like to be reconciled with my neighbor, but he has to make the first move." A friend contemplates the resolution of a longtime conflict. "After all, he wronged me. I did no wrong to him. He is the one who needs to express sorrow and request forgiveness. That is only right. Until he is ready to do that, we will just have to endure the discomforts of our division."

"Anybody can understand a person making one major mistake. But, three? That is another matter." A pastor is speaking about a parishioner. "Behavior of that kind stretches the limits of forgiveness. We just cannot go on and on forgiving such actions. We better dismiss her from our minds until she changes for the better, if she can, and proves it."

Conventional thoughts regarding forgiveness tend to be completely oblivious to Jesus' radical posture on this matter. Even within the church a propensity exists to forgive persons who are likeable and easily forgivable while treating other people, especially people involved in difficult situations, by other standards. Arguments to support such responses can sound very logical, "reasonable," even though they are non-biblical. On more than one occasion, Jesus reached out to people who refused to reach out to him. Jesus extended forgiveness to persons who had not even requested forgiveness.

According to the author of the Fourth Gospel, Jesus saved an adulteress from murder by a mob-inflicted justice. He forgave her and sent her on her way to a new life without the woman even so much as saying, "I'm sorry" initially or "thank you" before departing. In fact, Jesus appeared to be much more severe in his response to those people who had taken it upon themselves to judge and punish the woman for her wrongdoing than in his instruction to her despite her guilt.

Ponder Jesus' parable in which a father welcomes home a wayward, rebellious son. The son could be anyone. But, obviously the father is an image of God.

After mistreating his father, leaving home in an irresponsible rush, and living here and there slovenly, the son decided to return to his family. Evident in the biblical text of the story is the son's surmise that reinstatement in his father's household as a slave was about the best he could hope for. He knew, though, that even this acceptance would be contingent upon his careful confession of sin and recitation of sorrow. As the young man traveled homeward, he planned his approach to his offended father rehearsing over and over the litany of repentance that would be so important.

Two ingredients in this story no doubt shocked those who heard it first. When the father spotted his wayward son headed toward home, he set out running toward the young man. Not only was this action considered most undignified for a respectable Jewish patriarch, it seemed very unwise. The father should have made the boy come to him. In his eagerness for reconciliation, the old man struck out down the road toward his son before he even knew the young man's attitude. You just cannot afford to be too nice to that kind.

Second, the father granted forgiveness to the son before the son requested forgiveness from his father. Lavished, maybe stunned, by the love of his father, the sinful young man had no opportunity to declare his wrongdoing or to beg for forgiveness from anyone. All his rehearsals of a confession went for nought. At the very time when the prodigal son should have been penitently pleading his case in hopes of mercy, he was being fitted with garments of restoration and surrounded by symbols of celebration.

By far the gospel's most dramatic and unforgettable insight regarding forgiveness comes not from a parable but from a historical narrative. While on the cross, as he was dying, Jesus prayed to God for the forgiveness of those who put him there. He sought the gift of life for the very persons who were taking life from him.

Familiarity with this particular part of the execution scene must not be allowed to blunt the radicality of its meaning. Everybody knew what to expect from a man hanging on a cross. With whatever strength he has left, he screams words of rebuke, denunciation, and condemnation in the faces of those who placed him there. If an innocent man was crucified as guilty, even more piercing cries were predictable—loud protests of injustice and harrowing harangues about unfairness. Silence from a crucified sufferer was unthinkable. But, forgiveness? Silence interrupted only to speak of forgiveness? That scenario fell more into the category of unbelievable than unlikely.

Notice that Jesus' prayer for the forgiveness of his killers came from what was inside him, not because of the attitudes or the words of his executioners. Search the Gospel accounts of this sad spectacle. Where among the crucifixion crowd do you find a confession of sin, a statement of repentance, or a request for forgiveness? Yet, Jesus prayed, "Father, forgive them."

Sin has consequences that sinners cannot escape. However, true forgiveness does not continue condemnations and hurtful recriminations for the person forgiven.

A bank president—either willfully or unknowingly—mishandles some financial transactions. Colleagues assure him that they forgive him for what he has done though they cannot allow him to continue as the president of the bank. That is not forgiveness!

A church officer becomes involved in a relationship which some people criticize as indiscreet and others condemn as immoral. When she explains the specifics of the situation, members of the congregation respond by saying, "We love you and we forgive you. But we want you to leave our church. You no longer can serve as a leader here." That is not forgiveness!

Forgiveness is defined by scripture and modeled in the ministry of Jesus—not by culture, public relations experts, and "protect the organization at all costs" executives. In Jesus' parable, when the father forgave his disobedient, flagrantly evil son, he immediately restored the boy to full sonship (though the still-reeling boy gladly would have accepted the status of a slave). A historical fact, however, makes this point about forgiveness even more emphatically than this hortatory piece of fiction.

Peter—the once impressive fisherman turned impulsive, volatile disciple—denied Jesus! Loudly and harshly Peter disclaimed any association with Jesus, much less allegiance to him. What sin could be worse than that? Peter's negation of a personal relationship with Jesus came after his bold confession of Jesus as the Christ at Caesarea Philippi and his subjection to Jesus as the Savior during the footwashing in the Upper Room (earlier that same evening). No excuses. Peter knew of whom he spoke. Why Peter even had been warned of the possibility of facing a temptation to deny Jesus! Peter fully understood the severity of what he said. Peter sinned.

But that was not the end of the matter. No sooner had Jesus emerged from death as the risen Lord of all of life than he instructed two women to tell his disciples that he wanted to see them on a mountain top in Galilee. Not inconsequential, incidental, or accidental was the fact that in his instructions to the women, Jesus mentioned Peter by name—the only disciple he singled out by name. Though Peter had denied Jesus, Jesus wanted to be reunited with Peter. Peter was still in the group.

Once Jesus and the disciples were together again, the Lord commissioned Peter to serve as a leader in the primitive community of faith. Notice that questions typically pushed to the forefront in contemporary considerations of forgiveness did not receive any attention in the exemplary discussions of Jesus. (Did Peter display sorrow for what he had done? Had Peter made a formal statement of his wrongdoing and properly begged for forgiveness? What about a period of probation for Peter, to see if he can be trusted?) Jesus did not forgive Peter with any qualification about his personhood or reservation about his potential for servanthood. Forgiveness meant restoration.

Being ready to forgive and being thorough in forgiveness do not mean forgiveness is cheap and easy. God is always ready to forgive. God is always ready to forgive all sin. The same is true (or, should be) for all of God's people. The forgiveness available from God and commendable among the people of God, however, is as costly as it is difficult.

Witness again the painful murder of history's only totally innocent man—the crucifixion of the Incarnation of God. Self-evident is the difficulty—life sacrificially poured out to bring about good for people who at the very moment were laughing and joking their way through the most dastardly of evils. That particular price and difficulty are non-repeatable. But, forgiveness is always costly and painful.

How, then, does forgiveness occur? What makes forgiveness possible? Grace. The answer is grace. God's grace towards people. God's grace through people.

According to the gospel, forgiveness—a costly, comprehensive, compassionate, restorative act—is always available. Whenever, among whomever, and wherever sin occurs, forgiveness is a possibility. God authors it. God calls people to practice it.

13.
Centrality of Love

" . . . but the greatest of these is love." Paul the apostle wrote that conclusion after reflecting on the relationship between faith, hope, and love. Actually, though, this comment from the tentmaker from Tarsus would have been the same regardless of the components of his comparisons. When it comes to bottom lines in the gospel, none is more basic, more fundamental, more central than love.

Love is the means by which the divine-human relationship made possible through Christ best can be understood. Love characterizes the nature of interpersonal relationships as willed by God and modeled by Jesus. The essence of living as a Christian is living by love.

God is the source of love. One New Testament writer states the matter even more succinctly: "God is love" (1 John 4:16). Thus, love motivates every divine action. Love undergirds and pervades all that God has done and is doing in creation and redemption.

God's love defies reason and transcends explanation. God loves all people—every person—and wills what is best for each one. Irrelevant are judgments about whether or not a person is loveable or worthy of love. God loves everybody. Neither people's anger, disobedience, nor rebellion directed at God causes a cessation of God's love for those people. Even when someone is dead set on living in complete separation from God, in love God vigorously acts and patiently waits for reconciliation. Though often rejected, divine love is never defeated. God loves every person. Exceptions do not exist.

God, the God who is love, has no greater desire or no higher expectation than that people respond to the Divine Being and relate to other human beings in love. A bifocaled admonition about love occupies the heart of the Old Testament. The part of the Law that transcends every other part in importance instructs people to love God completely—with heart, soul, and strength—and to love their neighbors as they love themselves.

Redundant in the rhetoric of the ancient prophets is an emphasis upon love. According to those often fiery heralds of God's word, nothing pleases God like devoted love—not even personal sacrifices and temple rituals. God seeks genuine love from all people. Similarly, those advocates for righteousness announced that God's will for human relations is most fully realized when love dominates words and deeds.

Receiving God's love and returning God's love form the core of Christianity. Serious perversions of faith and devastating distortions of devotion develop when persons allow something other than love to become the bond between themselves and God.

Love forms the foundation and motivation for worshiping God. Worship is best understood not as a duty people have or an obligation to perform. Rather, worship is an opportunity for persons to know the exultation of expressing love and demonstrating devotion to the beloved Deity.

Stewardship is an important component of love. Who can imagine two lovers asking how much time they must spend with each other? Or inquiring about the minimum amount of money they have to devote to gifts for each other? Similarly, a person's stewardship of time, possessions, and all other aspects of life before God is not a dismal responsibility oriented to minimums. Responsible stewardship is a wonderful way for a person to reveal the depths of her love for God and thus realize the unfathomable joy of pleasing the One most loved.

Frequently, sharing faith with others or talking in public about a relationship to God has been commended as a means of avoiding guilt. "You ought to bear witness to your faith. You are guilty before God if you fail to do so." What a gross misunderstanding of witness or testimony. Again, the crucial issue is love. Who needs to be told to talk with others about the happiness of a fulfilling, life-transforming relationship of love? That is what witnessing is all about—a lover sharing with others the delightful news of his communion with the beloved.

A relationship with God never will be as fulfilling, meaningful, and joyful as possible as long as the basis of that relationship is guilt or duty. Or anything else other than love. God created people to be lovers. Lovers of God. Lovers of each other. Demonstrating such love, an individual becomes a true child of God and a mature human being.

A person's love for God, however, cannot be sustained in isolation from the rest of creation. A direct relationship exists between an individual's love for God and that individual's love for other people. Though that truth pervades all the literature in the New Testament, the author of 1 John states the matter bluntly: "Whoever does not love does not know God" (4:8). Just in case anyone might miss the sharp point of this statement or have any question about its application, only a few sentences later the same writer declares, "Those who say, 'I love God' and hate their brothers and sisters are liars; for those who do not love a brother or sister whom they have seen, cannot love God whom they have not seen" (4:20).

The unrivaled priority of love is presented with the greatest clarity imaginable, though, in the life and ministry of Jesus. Gospel writers repeatedly attempt to describe the breadth and depth of the Savior's compassion for all people. Jesus' unwavering intention that all people live in love for each other is unmistakable in their narratives.

Jesus made acting out of love for another person more important than conforming to specific statutes of the religious law. Almost too many times to number, Jesus' actions of love clashed with highly regarded religious regulations. Our chronological distance from the situation makes it very difficult for us to grasp the severity and volatility of Jesus' behavior.

The Sabbath was a sacred institution within Judaism, perhaps *the* most sacred institution in Judaism. Religionists devoted meticulous attention to how the Sabbath should properly be observed and preserved. Rules and regulations about keeping the Sabbath holy proliferated. No thoughtful person dared even question Sabbath laws much less tamper with them. Yet, Jesus elevated loving persons to a place of preeminence over maintaining institutions, including the institution of the Sabbath.

Early in his ministry, Jesus infuriated religious officials by healing a man with a withered hand on the Sabbath—a blatant breach of Sabbath regulations. Later, Jesus healed several other people on the Sabbath. Then, on another occasion Jesus broke a different part of Sabbath legislation in order to provide food for his hungry disciples. Jesus left no doubt regarding the conviction that undergirded his actions—the Sabbath is made for people, not people for the Sabbath.

Jesus considered the restoration of a ruptured relationship more important than participation in a specific service of corporate worship. He encouraged people going to worship while at odds with others to take a detour away from their places of worship in order to meet and to make peace with those with whom they had differences. Loving God and loving other people are integrally, inseparably related.

Those writers inspired by God to record the words and deeds of Jesus did not miss the high priority that he assigned to living by love. When the author of the Fourth Gospel commented on the entirety of Jesus' redemptive ministry, he explained it in terms of love, specifically as an extension of God's love—"For God so loved the world" (3:16). So that no one could ever misunderstand the nature of this love, the same writer explained that the central purpose of Jesus' loving mission was defined not by judgment and condemnation but by compassion and salvation.

According to Jesus, living by love is the most human way to live. Obviously, it is the divine way. People are to love each other in the same manner in which all persons have been loved by God.

In his well known story about a "good Samaritan," Jesus speaks of three persons' responses to a man in need. Readily apparent among the fictional characters are the conflicting motivations of real life—carefully prescribed duty versus the spontaneity of love, maintaining a schedule and keeping obligations versus expressing compassion and offering service. Jesus praises the person in his story who acts out of love and demonstrates mercy. Then, as he concludes his comments, Jesus says to all who listen and read, "Go and do likewise" (Luke 10:37). That means us.

Unfortunately, scores of people continue to understand religion (even Christianity) primarily in terms of duty and law. They fear God more than love God. They consider judgment superior to grace. They conceive of righteousness as static conformity to regulations rather than as dynamic expressions of love. Sadly, in every situation, adherents to this point of view care far more what the law dictates must be done than about what love declares can be done.

In this all-too-prevalent religious mind-set, being faithful resembles being miserable. People quietly assume that God surely would never approve of people doing what love leads them to do. In fact, a repression of feeling and thinking for one's self and a rejection of self-expression even in love are mistakenly identified as representations of the greatest kind of religious devotion. Popular perception holds suspect the very idea that the gospel really can be good news.

One word of qualification borders on a warning. Living by love is far more complicated and much more risky than living by law. Love requires action more than reaction. Lovers think creatively rather than practice obedience mechanically. And, such a life of love always has plenty of critics. Loud in voice and strong in number, duty-bound people laugh at lovers, scoff at them, and call them names. Reasonable people charge loving individuals with being out of touch with reality, naive in their belief that anyone can live by love in this world.

Vulnerability is a necessity and danger always a possibility in the lives of people who seek to live by love. The Pharisees lived as fanatically duty-bound individuals. They were good people in the worst sense of the word. Standing in sharp contrast to the Pharisees, not in terms of goodness but in his passion for grace, Jesus was a lover.

Interactions between these two, Jesus and the Pharisees, set a precedent that continues to be repeated. Adherents of a law-oriented, duty-bound religion worked so hard to do their religious duty that in the process they slaughtered perfect love. The brutal killing of Jesus murdered the incarnation of genuine compassion under the rubric of a law-defined righteousness practiced with religious devotion.

An apocryphal story about John the Apostle underscores the simplicity and centrality of love as a bottom line of the gospel. Legend has it that people had gathered to listen to what was to be the last sermon delivered by Saint John. Imagine the anticipation of not only hearing this great evangelist preach but receiving first hand the final distillation of his great wisdom. This giant in the faith was carried into the assembly as an old man. Out of the hush, he spoke of the essence of his experience.

With dignity and authority the elderly apostle said, "Little children, love one another." Immediately some listeners showed disappointment. Then, John repeated the words, "Little children, love one another." After a pause, he spoke precisely the same words again. And then again and again. In fact, those words constituted the entire content of John's sermon. Some folks were dismayed and considered it a shame that senility had reduced this great leader to such simplicity. However, others understood perfectly. The revered apostle had shared the very essence of his life-long reflection on the meaning of the gospel. "Little, children, love one another."

An argument can be made that these bottom lines of the gospel are so blatantly obvious that even a brief notation of them is needless— especially in a book on grace. The most of my life (a life intertwined with the institutional church), however, is evidence to the contrary. And, the strength of that prior religious posture is nowhere more in evidence than when seen in relation to grace.

I knew about the reality of sin. (My early religious models carried giant catalogues listing deplorable sinful actions, such as going to movies and playing cards.) But, I saw no remote relationship between sin and grace—subjects at opposite ends of a dichotomy. Forgiveness for sins was possible, of course. The reception of forgiveness was dependent, however, upon strict conformity to a ritual-like formula of request. Mess up in the manner of your confession of sin and you would miss out on the forgiveness of sin. Sure, I knew about the importance of love. But, even love was conditional. I cut my spiritual teeth on a religious mindset that feared more than loved God. Judgment seemed closer akin to righteousness than grace. People favored guilt over forgiveness as an effective spiritual motivator. Duty dominated freedom almost to the point of eliminating it entirely. Witnesses heralded salvation as a means of escaping Hell rather than experiencing abundant life.

The religious environment of my youth made the worship of God almost synonymous with "going to church" (little was said about what should happen once one was there). Everybody was expected to go to church or else to have to live with the horrible consequences of not attending. Sermons that earned the comment, "that's really preaching the Bible," consisted of a series of condemnations intended to send shudders of fear throughout members of the congregation. In fact, "Sunday services" were primarily experiences of receiving oratorically-hurled spears of judgment and wallowing in massive guilt. It all seemed like a proper penance for whatever had been done, though in reality not much of a deterrent to doing it all again.

My preparation for writing this chapter involves a huge segment of my lifetime. Even now as I affirm and commend the biblical reality of grace—the grace that can be discovered in a careful look at sin, forgiveness, and love as well as innumerable other subjects—I find myself thinking: "This is too good to be true; a community of grace seems like a figment of glorious fantasy." But, that is the very point of the gospel, is it not? God is so much better than most people think. The gospel really is good news.

Total elation is the proper response to a realization of God's gift of grace. But that is prevented by disturbing recognitions of the manner in which most people apply the gospel to life.

14.
Caveats of Redemption and Questions of Doubt

People may well reveal the true nature of their Christianity more in the words they speak after saying, "but" or "except" than in statements they make after declaring, "I believe." Orthodoxy is a snap in oral confessions. Lofty, creedal-like declarations cascade impressively across people's lips. Hymn texts praising gospel-shaped behavior can be sung heartily. Teachers in church schools stick strictly to lesson plans aimed at an accurate understanding of the ancient point of a biblical passage. However, application is absent. Many Christians pay little to no attention to how their spoken confessions, sung truths, and the scriptural principle studied specifically apply to complicated, troublesome contemporary situations. Here reservations appear. Discomfort develops. Nerve ceases to mean courage. Caveats of redemption abound.

But

"But." The word is as powerful as it is small. Inserted into the middle of a sentence, "but" can transform courage into cowardice, a substantive conviction into pitiable pablum, compassion into selfishness, redemption into retribution, and a church into just another social grouping within a community. Actions (or inaction) explained (or rationalized) by all-too-familiar litanies dominated by "but" deaden the integrity of faith and ruin the realization of communities of grace. Consider:

"I honestly want to live by the teachings of the Bible, *but* the writers of the Bible did not have to face the kinds of problems we must handle today."

"Certainly I believe Jesus' words about going a second mile, turning the other cheek, living by love, and practicing forgiveness, *but* even as Christians, especially as a church, we must be realistic, prevent questionable individuals from taking advantage of us, and guard against any vulnerability to misunderstanding and criticism."

"I want to help people as God commands, *but* I have no desire or intention to associate with, much less to assist, folks who could lead better lives and have fewer needs if they cared more and tried harder."

"We can accept divorcees as candidates for this position, *but* their marriages must have broken up prior to them becoming Christians."

"Our church should support social ministries, *but* we must take care not to leave an impression with the community that we support the lifestyles of those whom we serve."

"Living as a Christian is important to me, *but* I do not believe that means I have to approve of the construction of a rehabilitation unit in my neighborhood when such a development is sure to drive down property values."

"We desire always to be instruments of God's grace, *but* this family's problems are so publicly controversial that we best leave them alone."

"Ministers are right to assure people of God's love and grace as they address all kinds of evil, *but* I fear that so much positive talk makes it too easy on wrongdoers who need most to be challenged, reprimanded, and scared."

"It is one thing to forgive and support people who are so penitent that they seem almost pitiable, *but* I feel no responsibility whatsoever to forgive persons who after hurting me and embarrassing me still think they have rights and expect to be treated with dignity."

"I know Jesus accepted, forgave, and worked through people notorious for their immorality, *but* he did not have to worry about maintaining an institution as I do."

"Our congregation seeks to be open to all kinds of people and courageous in witness, *but* it makes no sense for us to go out and seek to enlist in our fellowship questionable characters who will make everybody else uncomfortable and maybe even drive away some of our more respectable members."

"Sure, the church of Christ should be different from other organizations, *but* we do not need to upset people in order to demonstrate our distinctiveness."

"I think I love all people as the Bible instructs, I really do, *but* my conscience demands that I condemn certain sins and, like it or not, I cannot do that without condemning as well the people who commit them."

"Those Christians who say people should not separate their public lives from their private lives and relegate faith to the private sector have a point, *but* the fact cannot be ignored that I must run my business by hard-nosed policies shaped by political realities, not by impractical, though nice-sounding, biblical ideals."

"I regularly pray for the improvement of people who have been imprisoned, *but* I refuse to support the designation of a single tax dollar for programs that make life better for them."

"Maybe the crucial question in every situation ought to be 'What would Jesus do?' *but* Jesus never faced the circumstances we must confront."

"But" was a word of great importance in the deeds-producing words of Jesus also. With what a difference though! Jesus uses the word "but" in the cause of redemption. Popular usage of the term in the present aims at establishing a caveat of redemption.

Jesus employs the conjunction "but" as a mode of *intensification*, not *exception* or *exemption,* in discussions of morality and grace. Repeatedly, in an almost formulaic fashion, Jesus takes the content of moral concerns far beyond actions prescribed by law. Jesus' interest focuses on the intentions and motivations that fill a person's heart—"You have heard that it was said . . . *But* I say to you" (Matt 5:21-48). When discussing the morality of killing, adultery, divorce, swearing, retaliation, and love, Jesus makes it clear that external action evaluated by religious legislation fades in importance compared to internal resolution. In the teachings of Jesus, keeping the letter of the law does not assure a life of love.

Jesus faced a multitude of "extenuating circumstances" that would justify his saying to the people involved, "I want to forgive you, *but*," "I want to accept you, *but*" or "I would like to help you, *but*." Not once, though, did that happen. Grace prevailed. Jesus never used the word "but" to narrow the realm of application, to restrict the extent of application, or to make a complete exemption of the exercise of grace. The only persons who did not receive grace from Jesus were individuals so insensitive to grace or resentful of grace that they either failed to accept it or actually rejected it.

Except

The term "except" possesses a power similar to that of "but." In discussions of interpersonal relations or institutional ministries, the presence of the word "except" can change everything dramatically. "Except" forms the grammatical glue used to hold together talk that points in one direction and behavior that moves in direct contradiction to the words spoken. "Except" acts as the linguistic bridge across which people move from statements of selfless intentions to rationalizations for selfish actions. "Except" serves as the oral connector by which one travels from affirmations of compassion to rejections of all that compassion demands. "Except" constructs a brick-wall-like barrier to realizations of the theological truth of grace.

People brandish about "except" as a term born of reason (and reason is considered more important than love). Thus, voicing "except" prevents individuals from making fools of themselves in support of a good cause. "Except" provides a piece of verbal camouflage that allows people to sound graceful without being graceful. "Except" is a cop-out on compassion; a caveat of redemption.

The term "except" takes on almost a liturgical nature because of its repetitive presence in religious discussions related to difficult, desperate-for-grace situations. Consider:

"Love should prevail in all circumstances *except* those in which reason contradicts love."

"As parents, we want our child to be obedient to God's will *except* in considering missions involvements that would place her amid the most undesirable people in the city."

"Today's church must find ways to re-enact the compassionate outreach of our Lord toward contemporary 'lepers' *except* where victims of AIDS are present."

"Our ministry to families is extended without restrictions *except* in cases where a family unit is known to contain abused members."

"We want to provide the very best in Christian education to all who are interested *except* to persons with physical, mental, or emotional handicaps."

"In our church's program of discipleship training, we welcome everybody *except* a person whose bad reputation could be a negative influence on our evangelistic outreach."

"Every sin is forgivable *except* intentional sin; if you knew what you were doing when you did wrong, don't expect any understanding or help from me."

"Jesus' teachings in the Sermon on the Mount should be taken literally and obeyed carefully *except* in the realms of economics and government."

"God's grace needs the strongest possible emphasis *except* among people who may be prone to confuse grace with license."

While visiting in Kenya, a minister-friend who lives there told me of a common problem among native converts to Christianity. When confronted by a crisis, they often revert to primitivism. As long as life goes well for these folks, their newfound faith seems strong. Trouble, however, precipitates a panicked return to pre-conversion practices (reliance upon a witch doctor and conformity to other more pagan tribal traditions).

Is that not a dramatization of how people seek to avoid Christian redemption by the verbalization of "except"? Is God's grace to be the very foundation of our existence only until we face difficulties? Do crises justify a lack of compliance with the fundamentals of biblical redemption?

Questions and Doubts

What is it with Christianity? Is grace only for the good times? If basic Christian truths do not apply in the face of turbulent troubles as well as in periods of near normalcy, surely their validity must be questioned. Is hope to be affirmed everywhere except in a juvenile detention facility? Is the power of faith in a person's life to be believed except in relation to a man whose character is viewed with suspicion? Can the church forgive the sin and accept the ministry of a woman guilty of murder but not of adultery? Is restorative grace available only to those folks who promise never to take advantage of it? Are discussions of love for others to be set aside if gossip makes such dialogues the objects of condemnation? Is a run-away young person to be exempted from the church's understanding and encouragement? Is Christian fellowship to be withheld from families hurt by divorce or extended only to the most innocent partner in a broken marriage? Is a homeless, hungry man to be denied a hot meal because of the odor of alcohol in his breath?

Handling theoretical matters is a breeze for most people. Not so relational concerns. And, there is the problem. Some of my most soul-harrowing doubts arise not because of disturbing new insights related to the Bible or controversial publications on the doctrinal positions of respected theologians. Most often, the actions of flesh and blood people, rather than the assertions of abstract principles, throw into question my cherished beliefs. Broken promises, betrayals, disappointments, anger, selfishness, and hard-heartedness relationally can shape a powerful sense of failure and defeat theologically. I am not alone.

"It doesn't work!" a dejected, lonely woman screams in response to a declaration of belief in the gospel. An abused business man scorns, "Nobody can live by love and grace in this kind of world. Those priorities create an insane vulnerability sure to result in incredible hurt." A victim of vicious community gossip, surprisingly devoid of an understandable bitterness, asks in sincerity, "What's the use? If redemptive action is not forthcoming when life has bottomed-out, when on earth is it to be expected? If grace is nowhere to be found in a situation in which grace is needed everywhere, what is the point of grace?"

At first glance, such comments and questions appear to be classic symptoms of a crisis of belief. Not so. The real doubt-precipitating problems are best identified by their first and last proper names, not by theological labels. People are the problems. Hurting, doubting individuals realize that the persons deepening their difficulties and increasing their burdens are reputably "good" folks who fervently avow their belief in redemption. Ironically (as well as sadly and tragically), troubled people all-too-often discover that a refuge, a community of grace and redemption, is not available in a fellowship that ostensibly prizes both redemption and grace.

Personally, convictions clash with observations. I believe the gospel to be a sufficient guide in all situations. No reasons for compromise exist within the Christian faith. Hope finds no obstacles that are insurmountable. Love has no limits. Grace knows no exceptions. However, I cannot ignore the proliferation of caveats of redemption that throw into question the very reality of redemption (not from God, but among people).

During a difficult period in my life, disillusionment and depression assaulted my confidence in persons and provoked doubts about the possibility of a community of grace. At that time, I wrote in my journal: "All I have thought to be important in life doesn't work, or if it does work for a while, it doesn't last long. Maybe none of it is true. Even individuals who say all of the right words and affirm basic beliefs with which I concur cannot be counted on in a crunch. Crises drive us to a primitivism in which passionately watching out for one's own best interests prevails over all else."

This brief literary look at hedging on compassion, making conditional that which is supposed to be unconditional, using good words to justify good-less actions, and designating exemptions from redemption is enough to cause a person either completely to give up on any pursuit of a community of grace or honestly to ask, "Just what is grace anyway?" The fact that this book continues with more chapters reveals my basic disposition on this matter.

I want to take a stab at answering that question about the nature of grace.

IV.
The Gift of Grace

"The gift of grace is not a reward for hard work or good behavior, it is a lark, a joke, a hilariously inequitable largesse: it is, in a word, a gift."

Robert Farrar Capon
Parables of Judgment

"Those who try to deal with God by bargaining, by demanding favor to which they have earned a right through their own good deeds, by winning his mercy and forgiveness through their own efforts . . . are confounded and fall on their faces. While those who have no right to mercy or love . . . are astonished and swept up in irresistible and overwhelming grace."

Andrew M. Greeley
Ascent Into Hell

"Grace" is one of those realities about which people say, "I know what it is, but I don't have words to describe it. Grace is hard to explain." A friend speaks of the city in which he is a new resident as a "place of grace." Paul Tillich, the internationally renowned theologian-philosopher, writes of "gestalts of grace." A young woman reflects on an uplifting conversation with a counselor and describes it as a "moment of grace." Andrew Greeley, the popular priest-sociologist-author, describes his novels as "parables of grace." After a Sunday morning congregation sings the old gospel song "Amazing Grace," a minister stands behind a pulpit and declares that the whole of Christianity is to be understood as a "life of grace." Thomas Acquinas, the formative genius of Catholic theology, described grace as "a supernatural somewhat."

What is grace?

Recognizing grace is much easier than talking about grace. Discussing grace in generalities is less difficult than forming specific definitions of grace. Most problematic, though, is exercising grace. Not surprisingly, words praising grace far exceed acts implementing grace.

Obviously, people cannot form a community of grace apart from an adequate understanding of grace. Such comprehension requires great care. Mistaken identity is easy.

Impostors of a community of grace abound. Numerous fellowships talk the language of grace, take on the adornments of grace, and display a printed pledge of allegiance to the goals of grace. But, entrance into these communities is like passing through the door of a fake storefront on a movie set. The facade is perfect—it looks like the real thing—but nothing is behind it. From the street everybody is impressed. After moving inside, however, disappointment prevails.

Constructing a helpful community of grace necessitates understanding the biblical meaning of grace.

15.
What's in a Word?

The English word "grace" literally translates the Latin term *gratia,* an equivalent to the Greek noun *charis.* At the root of the Latin word is an adjective *ratus*, which means "pleasing," clearly an antecedent to contemporary thought that associates grace with a pleasure, a favor, or an attractive, impressive display of physical skills ("She danced with great grace.")[11] The Greek term derives from *chairein* which means "to rejoice." Thus, grace and joy or delight are closely related.[12]

Pay careful attention to casual conversations and you will hear the word "grace" used for multiple purposes and employed to describe diverse actions. Some people equate grace and goodwill—either in the offering of a gift or the expression of gratitude from one who receives a gift. Grace can be written or voiced as a greeting or as an indication of best wishes at the time of a farewell. Not uncommonly, individuals associate grace with charm or use it as a description of beautiful trinkets or as an observation about a person's gratifying behavior. Both in ancient secular Greek as well as in contemporary society, grace appears closely related to "favor"—the attractiveness as well as the substance of a favor extended to another and the thankfulness with which a favor is accepted.

Grace takes on distinctive content within the literature of the Bible and the thought of Christianity. Two important word pictures from the Old Testament comprise a strong foundation upon which to erect a New Testament definition of the term. The Hebrew root of the word translated "grace" in the Old Testament means literally "to bend down." The image is that of a concerned parent bending down to help a hurting, helpless child. The other Hebrew term solidly behind the word "grace" is most often translated "loving kindness" or "steadfast love."[13] Old Testament writers employ both of these concepts in writing about the grace of God, identifying grace as utterly self-giving action prompted solely by love.

New Testament writers describe "grace" more than they define it. Their various glimpses of grace can be combined to form a rather comprehensive picture of grace.

Grace is a gift. Not a reward for doing good, rather a divinely-provided means of moving toward "good" (a quality unattainable by a person acting apart from God and alone). Grace transcends law. Grace is not contingent upon obedience. Salvation comes by grace. Grace enables persons to accomplish special spiritual tasks to perform. Grace summarily describes the entire status of a Christian.[14]

Specifics are important. The source of grace is God. The medium of grace is Jesus Christ. Through the life and ministry of Jesus, divine grace touches human need. God's grace motivated and undergirded the coming of Jesus. Indeed, Jesus personifies, humanly defines, grace. Jesus embodies the grace he mediates and commends to others.

Among contemporary Christian thinkers, efforts to address the meaning of grace tend more toward observations, illustrations, and metaphorical allusions than succinct definitions. Descriptive statements about grace far outnumber synonyms for grace or prescriptions of grace's content. In reality, no one comment alone can serve as a satisfactory definition of grace. An adequate understanding of grace needs the information provided by numerous different insights regarding its multiple dimensions.

In a recent book that heralds grace as "the final word, the eternal word," William Boggs describes grace as "the very practical, life-oriented dimension of love."[15] From the much respected wisdom of Reinhold Niebuhr comes an older comment asserting that "Grace is every impulse or power that operates against the pull of my self-regard, and makes me truly a self by helping me to forget myself."[16] Other statements about grace more explicitly recognize its divine source. C. L. Mitton refers to grace as "God's uncovenanted, undeserved mercy toward man in Jesus."[17] Similarly, David Harned says, "Grace means a gift unexpected and undeserved, God with man and for him."[18] In a very fine sermon from several decades ago, the revered Scottish preacher James Stewart isolates the two basic components of grace—grace is God's initiative (love goes into action first) for the undeserving (people with no merit).[19]

Frederick Buechner refers to grace as that "power beyond all power, the power that holds all things in manifestation . . . a Christ-making power . . . a power that makes Christ . . . a power that works through the drab and hubbub of our lives to make Christs of us."[20] (Implicit in Buechner's words is the embryonic idea of a community of grace—a community that is not only the body of Christ but a fellowship of Christs.) With similar sentiments, Robert Capon relates grace to hearing music, not listening for errors by the musician. Capon calls grace a power that can make even infirmities occasions of glory. He concludes that grace is the celebration of life relentlessly hounding all the non-celebrants in the world.[21]

So much for attention to the word "grace." None of the disciplines of philology can produce the whole story about grace. An understanding of the distinctive nature of grace within Christianity requires serious Bible study.

16.
Textual Truths

Grace is predominantly a New Testament word. More specifically, grace is primarily a Pauline word within the New Testament. Of the 152 times the term "grace" (*charis*) appears in the New Testament, 101 of the occurrences are attributable to the apostle Paul. Of the 51 other uses of "grace" in the non-Pauline works, over half of them (27) are in Acts and 1 Peter, literature closely associated with Paul.[22]

In the synoptic Gospels, the word "grace" appears only in Luke (6 times). The author of the Fourth Gospel limits his use of the term to the Prologue (3 times). In the epistles of 1 John, 3 John, and Jude, the word "grace" is not used.

Helpful insights into the meaning of grace arise from a careful study of the biblical texts in which the word "grace" actually appears. Not every such text has to receive intense scrutiny, however. In numerous New Testament passages, "grace" is present as a means of greeting (e.g. Rom 1:7) or a term of farewell (e.g. Rom 16:20).[23] Paul uses the word "grace" in this dual manner in all of his letters. Also, occasionally a writer employs the term "grace" to express "thanks" (e.g. 2 Cor 8:16). These specialized usages of the word "grace" do not contribute significantly to an understanding of the substance of grace and an application of its meaning.

Even a quick scan of other New Testament texts that contain the word "grace" reveals the beneficial-for-understanding possibilities of the kind of subject-oriented studies that follow. The textual analyses below are not intended to be comprehensive so much as representative (indicative) and provocative.

One constant is apparent. Basic to every biblical statement on grace (regardless of the related subjects involved) is the presupposition that grace is a gift—a gift from God. Antecedents of this New Testament truth reside in the Old Testament scriptures. There writers consider grace as certain as God's being because they recognize grace as an important dimension of the divine nature. Outside factors cannot alter this reality. Repeatedly, ancient thinkers tell how God's grace finds expression in the face of people's disobedience and faithlessness toward God. The apostle Paul stands on the shoulders of his predecessors in the faith as he elaborates the truth that grace comes as a gift from God (Rom 3:24; Eph 2:8, 3:7, 4:7; 2 Cor 9:14-15).

Allowing the giftedness of grace to sink in to the wonder of the soul is an important prelude to the study of any scriptural text on grace. Dismiss the idea of making "good sense" of grace. Grace defies human reason. Merit is not even in the picture. Worth is disregarded similarly.

All thoughts of earning grace or purchasing grace are just causes for hilarious laughter—contributors to a comedy spontaneously formed in response to the utterly ridiculous. Anyway grace is observed, studied, or explained, grace is a gift. Anybody interested in learning about grace (or knowing more about grace) who cannot start here—with grace as a gift—cannot start at all.

Jesus: Grace Upon Grace
(John 1:16-17; Rom 1:5; 2 Cor 8:9ff.)

The best way to learn the most about grace is to look at Jesus. Jesus is grace—the product of God's grace, the medium of God's grace, and the incarnation of God's grace. Within the ministry of Jesus, grace is redundant. Commenting on Jesus, the author of the Fourth Gospel writes not just of grace but of "grace upon grace."

Paul discusses the essential meaning of the Incarnation in terms of grace. In a manner reminiscent of the magnificent kenotic passage in Philippians 2:6-11, Paul tells his Corinthian readers how Jesus gave up richness and embraced poverty so that the poor could become rich. The apostle metaphorically uses words commonly associated with economics to convey a spiritual truth.

The Incarnation was an act of divine sacrifice, self-emptying. Jesus gave up the benefits of perfection in order that all people might have an opportunity to experience salvation; Jesus forfeited the glories of heaven to live amid the hell of this earth so that the perpetrators of the "hell" might be able to know the joys of heaven. Why? Why would God do that? Why would Jesus choose such submission? Grace! "Grace" is the answer to all three of those questions. The only answer.

Divine compassion has nothing to do with human desserts. Redemption is not an effort to return a favor. All of the actions of Jesus are expressions of grace. Jesus is grace.

Attempts to depict Jesus as someone other than the incarnation of grace are plentiful. And harmful. Such efforts emerged at the inception of Jesus' ministry. They persist into the present. Jesus was not a new

Moses-like lawgiver, a kingly policy-maker, or a military mind-shaper. Jesus did not establish a code of ethics that has to be followed, a narrow vocabulary that has to be verbalized, a religious ritual that has to be repeated, a doctrinaire creed that has to be confessed, or a formula for decision-making that has to be implemented for one to be acceptable to God. Jesus demonstrated the possibilities of a life of grace and extended to everyone an invitation to enjoy it.

At the eye of the storm of controversy that swirled around Jesus was the issue of grace. Many people, especially religionists, did not want even to hear Jesus' message of grace much less practice his ministry of grace (as beneficiaries or emissaries). But, they did not deter Jesus. Individuals could reject grace if that was their preference. Rejection from some, however, did not terminate Jesus' offer of grace to others—to all.

Nowhere is the intensity of some folks' hostility toward grace more obvious than in the crucifixion of Jesus. At that killing place outside of Jerusalem (though it could have been anywhere, anytime), "good" people with admirable convictions violently acted out their conviction that grace cannot form the center of religion. Angry, but supposedly religious, resisters wanted Jesus out of their world. They believed that grace has no place in the affairs of humans. The very moment of people's ultimate protestation about grace, however, became the occasion for history's most profound demonstration of grace. Jesus did what his murderers were betting their lives could not be done. Exercising grace even as he died, Jesus used the worst moment possible to accomplish the greatest good imaginable. Jesus met condemnation and rejection with an invitation to salvation.

True disciples of Jesus do not practice the kind of religion that brought about his crucifixion. To accept Jesus means to receive grace. To follow Jesus means to live by grace. Christians are agents of grace whether in a one-on-one relationship with an individual or amid the social structures of a community.

The Gospel of Grace
(Acts 14:3, 20:24, 32)

If the reason for the gospel is Jesus, and if Jesus is the incarnation of grace, the gospel is the good news about grace. That is precisely what Paul preaches—the gospel of grace. And, that is how Luke describes the

content of Paul's preaching. Also, the gospel of grace is the content of
Jesus' words and actions.

What is the gospel? This simple question has spawned numerous and
diverse responses. Some people equate the gospel with a set of
theological propositions to be believed. Others argue that the gospel is a
particular perspective on life to be assumed. Still others conceive of the
gospel as a code of behavior to be adopted.[24] But, none of these attempts
at defining the gospel coincides with the understanding of the gospel that
is basic to the New Testament. The correct answer to this inquiry about
the meaning of the gospel is crucial since believing (faithing) the gospel
is the human act by which salvation is embraced.

Biblically speaking, the gospel is a person—Jesus of Nazareth.
Whether stated traditionally as in Matthew, pastorally as in Mark, theo-
logically as in Luke, or philosophically as in John (the four "Gospels"),
the gospel centers on the advent of Jesus—the Messianic "son of David"
(Matthew), "the Son of God" (Mark), the son of Mary (Luke), and the
"Word (that) was God" (John). This person, Jesus, incarnates grace.

To believe in the gospel means to believe in (to accept, to have faith
in, to follow) Jesus, the embodiment of grace. To proclaim the gospel
means to tell about Jesus, which is to speak of grace. To live by the
gospel means to attempt to live as Jesus lived, which is to be governed
by grace.

Some people are always uneasy with such stark simplicity. Look at
the matter historically. Efforts come and go to make the message of
Christianity embrace something more than the gospel. Evangelists say to
those seeking salvation: "You must accept these five spiritual laws,"
"You must not break any of these eight commandments," or "You must
conform to this particular lifestyle." Self-appointed defenders of God act
"to preserve righteousness" (because to say "believing the gospel" is just
not to say enough to guarantee what they demand), seek to make conditional that which Jesus made unconditional, to relate to merit that
which Jesus knew never could be merited, and to restrict protectively that
which Jesus made available to all freely and compassionately. All such
attempts to distort the gospel deserve the same kind of stern rebuke Paul
levels at any person proclaiming a "different" gospel or "another" gospel
among the Galatians—"let that one be accursed" (1:9).

Only one gospel exists. Jesus gives it content. The good news from
God is the gospel of grace. In any situation, if the gospel is present, so

is grace. Conversely, in any situation, if grace is absent, so is the gospel. No gospel, no grace. No grace, no gospel!

Salvation by Grace
(Rom 3:24, 5:1-2, 20; Eph 2:5)

Serious Bible study can alter history. Witness the scripture-prodded reformation in the sixteenth century! Serious Bible study can change a person's life completely. Read the life stories of innumerable persons like C. S. Lewis who were "surprised by joy"! Nowhere is the potency of the Bible's message more self-evident than in passages that address the subject of salvation.

Paul is the New Testament's primary writer-interpreter regarding salvation. Both what he says and how he says it reflect the backdrop against which he writes, the context in which he ministers, and the audience he addresses. This remarkable apostle confronts numerous, at times seemingly insurmountable, misunderstandings of the nature of salvation. Among Jewish-oriented persons, some related salvation to the perpetuation of certain traditions, conformity to rabbinic legislation, and even the adoption of cultural components of Judaism. In the Greek world, people attempted to wed salvation to various mythological precepts or philosophical ideas. By way of response, Paul states succinctly, but forcefully, what salvation is. He leaves no question about what salvation is not.

Salvation is by grace through faith. No more. No less.

Salvation comes from God. Only! To know salvation a person must receive it from God as a gift. The only reason salvation is available at all is because of grace—the grace of God. That is it. Salvation talk has no place in it for assertions about what a person deserves or commentaries about an individual's goodness or evil. Salvation comes from God, not because of who people are or what people have done but because of who God is.

Morality is important, very important, in the life of every person. The nature of an individual's morality, however, is not a contingency upon which the possibility of salvation depends. In the New Testament, the opposite of sin is faith, not virtue. Robert Capon states the matter correctly even if, in the opinions of some people, controversially: "Our morals have nothing to do with either our salvation or our damnation. We are saved only because God, immorally, has accepted us while we are yet sinners; and we are damned only if we stupidly, . . . insist on rejecting that acceptance by unbelief. . . . It's Jesus . . . who makes all the difference."[25] Capon further asserts that salvation is a result of saying yes to Jesus in faith. Neither the emotional intensity of the confession nor the actional reforms attached to it affect its validity. "Nothing ever matters—nothing ever will matter—but faith."[26]

Faith—people's faith—is essential in the experience of salvation. But even human faith depends upon divine grace. Unaided by God, no one can meet the expectation of God. However, that is not a problem. Graciously, God gives to people what is requested from people—faith. Faith is the God-provided means by which a person can accept the God-offered gift of salvation. Of course, God respects human freedom. Every individual has the liberty to reject grace and deny faith, thus choosing to live apart from salvation. In reality, though, even this provision of the divine sovereign is an act of grace.

With all of his heart and mind, Paul believed in the sole sufficiency of God's grace accepted in faith as the means of salvation. With all of his might throughout all of his ministry, this apostle rigorously sought to defeat all views to the contrary. Grace and faith need no supplements—neither Jewish circumcision nor Gnostic wisdom, animal sacrifices, or personal achievements.

Ironically, though few, if any, other textual truths receive as much careful attention and vocal elaboration as this one, the radicality of its importance and relevance is blunted when it is translated into life. Grace needs no supplements. But, look at history. A tendency exists to make salvation dependent upon something more than grace—whether the specifics are purchases of ecclesiastical indulgences in the sixteenth century or obedience to cultural mores in the twentieth century. God will not stand for that. Anyone, including religious leaders, or any group, including churches, who makes the basis of salvation anything other than a person's faith response to the gift of God's grace exhibits infidelity to God's Word as revealed in the gospel.

Law and Grace
(Matt 5:17; Rom 6:14-15, 11:6)

The advent of Jesus altered everything. Controversy ensued. Jesus' treatment of the law whipped up cyclonic conflicts that surrounded him everywhere he went.

Speaking and acting with authority, Jesus changed the traditional status of the law as established by the religious community. In no sense did Jesus abolish the law. But in every sense, Jesus moved beyond the law. Jesus knew that the spiritual quality of a life motivated by law never can come close to the exemplary nature of a life nurtured by grace. More than once, Jesus made clear that even legalistic perfection (if that were a possibility) falls short of the expectation of God revealed in divine affirmations of salvation by grace.

Prior to the coming of Christ, obedience to the law was considered the ultimate criterion by which people could judge the strength of each other's relationship with God. Jesus removed the law from this role and replaced it with grace. But the factor of human judgment was not replaced with anything. Jesus did not want people judging each other. A devotion to grace decimates a person's desire to pass judgments on others.

To say that many people preferred law to grace as the sovereign spiritual value is an understatement. The crucifixion of Jesus bombastically declares that truth. Innumerable individuals were hooked on a performance-based religion measured by law. They panicked to the point of committing murder to prevent the emergence of a religion motivated by grace and committed to liberation. All around the cross of Christ stood persons so fearful of a law-transcending good that they were eager to do evil to preserve their kind of good. The good that they protected, though, was infinitely inferior to the good that they willed to eradicate.

Once he embarked on his ministry as a Christian apostle, Paul stayed in the middle of continuing controversy about the law. Representative of his convictions about the relationship between law and grace are Paul's straight-forward words to his readers in Rome (Rom 6:14-15). What the apostle said then remains of great significance now.

Only by a careful study of the tenses of Paul's verbs can a reader of his letters decide when Paul is writing about the future and when he is focusing on the present. Often Paul refers to future conditions as if they were present realities. Numerous interpreters read Romans 6:14-15 in this manner—pushing the truths of the passage into the future. They insist that Paul's words about the sovereignty of grace describe a situation that someday will exist for all believers. But not now. Only Paul's remarks about a Christian's freedom from the dominion of sin are considered of current relevance. That interpretation is wrong. Clearly, the apostle's words are written in the present tense. Paul is pointing to a present reality—"You are not under law but under grace."

Paul anticipates (or repeats) the question that his critics raise in response to this assertion. "Are we to sin because we are not under law but under grace?" In so doing, he reveals a major flaw in the mindset of a typical legalist.

Freedom born of grace scares legalists half to death. They mistakenly assume that only the law can prevent sin, that righteousness can be measured accurately only in terms of obedience to the law, and that without the law people will want to sin more. How negative! How distrustful of the power of the gospel of grace! Note the unusual forcefulness of Paul's reaction: "By no means." ("God forbid!" is the force of the apostle's words.)

Paul knew what his legalistic antagonists needed to discover. Grace deals sin a death-blow much more effectively than does law. People motivated by grace desire to do far more good than the law commands and seek to avoid evils that the law fails to forbid.

Conformity to the law determines virtue when human efforts become prerequisites to righteousness. The ineptness (and sometimes wickedness) of such a religion has been exposed enough for all people to know better. But often, the law functions as a major source of security. Thoughts of what would happen if the sovereignty of the law were removed provoke a desperate, insane clinging to commandments. That was the situation confronted by Paul (even as earlier by Jesus).

Though some people eventually saw that human obedience to the law never could be the basis of salvation, they still retained obedience to the law as the essential measurement of character among the saved. They offered grace to non-believers as the only means of salvation but retained conformity to the law as the only acceptable evidence of salvation. Conversely, Paul identifies grace not only as the one foundation for salvation but as the major guide to be followed in the lives of the saved.

Paul was not an antinomian ready to discard the law altogether. In fact, Paul wrote about the law with profound appreciation for it. By no stretch of the imagination did Paul ascribe to lawless behavior. However, Paul knew the limitations of the law. The law can judge everybody, but it cannot save anybody. The law is excellent for facilitating condemnation among persons, but it is impotent in affecting transformation in a person. Such knowledge was the source of the passion with which Paul wrote about the primacy of grace.

Legalists remain plentiful. Most (but certainly not all) have given up on a legally-defined works theology of salvation and vigorously advocate salvation by grace alone. Far too many of them, however, continue to turn only to the law for an understanding of righteousness. They praise grace at the moment of salvation. But, after that, they replace grace with law.

Often, legalists leave the impression that grace is available only once. With a spirit of love, they invite people to experience salvation by grace and to know forgiveness for their sins. After conversion, though, look out! They put grace away. When sin occurs among the redeemed, the response is harsh judgment based solely upon law.

Performance-bound Christianity develops out of a legally-defined spirituality. Both the church and the world are full of it. Typically, a performance-based orientation to life breeds sickness emotionally and spiritually. On the one hand is an unhealthy pride born of unrealistic expectations about one's self. On the other hand is a disturbingly low self-esteem fostered by failed attempts to achieve perfection.

Among believers preoccupied with performance, grace recedes in importance. Their attention turns almost exclusively to human efforts. Unfortunately, in this situation destructive evils can emerge amid a mad pursuit of some elusive good. David Seamands adeptly describes what happens:

> A virtue becomes a vice. An ideal is turned into an idol. A reality becomes a counterfeit. A gift to be received we try to achieve. The search for excellence twists into a struggle for supremacy. An undeserved relationship distorts into deserved one-upmanship. The empty, open hand becomes a grasping, clenched fist.[27]

Protests to the contrary aside, to be for grace is not to be against law. John Oman explains that grace takes seriously people's legal relation to

God by removing the legal dimension from that relation.[28] An affirmation of grace is not an invitation to licentiousness.

In reality, grace takes morality more seriously than does the law. Action in conformity to a commandment is not enough alone to guarantee moral integrity. The substance of true righteousness involves the mind, heart, and deed in a union of love devoted to the best interest of others and to the glorification of the God of grace.

Grace in Society
(2 Pet 3:18; Eph 4:29; Col 4:6; 2 Cor 8:7-9, 19)

Grace is no "ivory tower" doctrine valuable only in theological discussions and applicable to "purely spiritual" issues. Grace is a personal concern, but not a private one. Grace involves much more than a good attitude, wishful thinking about well-being, and admirable intentions. Grace is a way of life in which God's love for a person becomes the model by which that individual relates to other people.

The apostle Paul urges continuous growth in grace among all Christians. Mature spirituality and a generosity of grace are inseparable. Individuals should allow the gift of grace received from God so to saturate their lives that grace dominates all their thoughts, words, and acts. Lest anyone consider grace an irrelevant "spiritual ambiguity," Paul illustrates the practicality of grace within society with specifics.

Speech reveals the presence (or absence) of grace in a person's life. At issue here is not talking *about* grace, but speaking *with* grace. A person's words are to "minister grace" to all who hear them. Characteristically, instruments of grace build-up, not tear down; help and heal, not hurt or destroy; convey understanding compassion, not unleash harsh condemnation. So it goes with words of grace.

But, these observations do not get to the real guts of grace. Anyone can speak graciously to admired friends and respected acquaintances who seem never to do any wrong. The real test of grace in communication comes in relation to individuals who are not liked; persons whose behavior is a source of aggravation, disgust, disappointment or anger; folks who hold controversial ideas; and group members in conflict. Specifically, grace-filled speech rejects words of rumor, gossip, judgment, suspicion, and depreciation; words that hurt other people cause a breach in fellowship, and disrupt community. Words of grace offer support,

encouragement, forgiveness (if needed), and an assurance of unconditional, active love.

Note carefully the context of Paul's admonition about speaking with
grace in Colossians. Paul has in mind conversations with pagans, not
Christians. The much-traveled apostle commends grace-full speech directed toward persons who would not necessarily deserve it, understand it,
or return it.

Prominent among the first readers of Paul's instructions were new
Christians who could justify fanatical hostility toward pagans as an indication of their admirable fidelity to Christ. Paul warns against such talk.
Related to other people's lives, rabid condemnations, loosely-spoken
judgments, and oral invasions into private realms are morally wrong as
well as woefully inappropriate. In no situation is a Christian to speak of
another person—any other person—in a way that is less than friendly and
gracious. Speaking as a Christian means speaking as a sympathetic
friend.

Oral communication is very important, but so is social action. That
is the second realm in which Paul's conviction about grace finds practical
application. Grace goes beyond speech. In his writings, Paul uses precisely the same word to describe the source of salvation from God and
the financial collection taken for the needy people in Jerusalem—grace
(*charis*). That which provides salvation for sinners is identical with that
which precipitates help for the poor—unmerited favor, aggressive goodness. The former comes directly from God. The latter is a gift from God
delivered through God's people.

Initially, the recipients of "2 Corinthians" were Gentile Christians.
Apart from Paul, they had no first hand contact with the believers in
Jerusalem for whom a charitable offering was being taken. In fact, if the
Corinthians knew anything at all about the people in need, likely they
were aware that the Jerusalem Christians were pro-Jewish and anti-
Gentile in their approach to Christianity, thus folks probably cool to the
major sentiments of their fellowship. Yet, Paul identifies financial assistance from the Christians in Corinth for the hungry in Jerusalem as an
outgrowth of grace.

True to the nature of grace, Paul addresses his readers with counsel
rather than a commandment. As much as this compassionate apostle
longed to see help offered to the people in Jerusalem, he wanted the
Corinthians to act out of character-building grace, not a commandment-

induced obedience. (Grace is a redemptive response to a personal need, not strict conformity to a legal demand.) An offering collected in this manner would be a thorough-going act of grace. As James Reid explains in his exposition of this passage of scripture, "Liberality with love behind it is the work of grace in those who give; and it is the work of grace on those who receive."[29]

True beneficiaries of grace become generous benefactors of grace. Those who have sinned, who have been abused and victimized, who have known deceit and disgrace, and then discovered grace cannot be restrained from offering grace to others who are overwhelmed with similar experiences. Grace received is a dynamic impulse that can be satisfied only as grace is distributed. Grace will not permit idleness as long as any segment of society remains deprived of food, health, education, clothing, shelter, and freedom. When social structures themselves become barriers to the realization of these bare minimums for all persons, those structures become targets for destruction by conspirators with grace. Ministry and grace are inseparable. Grace is forever busy in services to hurting people and efforts to accomplish the greatest good possible in the establishment of true community.

17.
Reading between the Lines

So far, the biblical meaning of grace has been explored only in relation to New Testament passages in which the word "grace" actually appears. More study is needed. Many of the most profound scriptural truths about grace are revealed in texts that do not contain the term "grace." In the Bible, insights into the nature of grace far outnumber appearances of the word itself.

In a sense, the entirety of the Bible elaborates the meaning of grace. Old Testament passages regarding God's election of Israel, the divine deliverance of the Israelites from Egypt, and God's provisions for the chosen people, despite their countless rebellions against God, provide rich resources for understanding the nuances of grace. Those people did not merit God's goodness. Divine mercy came only as a response to human need. That is grace.

In the New Testament, passages on grace abound. Though the word "grace" scarcely can be found in the Gospels, indisputably grace constitutes the theme of the Gospels. Reporting and reflecting on the life of Jesus requires writing about grace. In addition to the numerous Pauline texts on grace already considered, much more material on grace is available in the writings of this pioneer apostle.

As a conclusion to this brief biblical study of grace, a few additional grace-oriented passages from the New Testament will be considered. Though the word "grace" does not appear in any of these texts, insights into the nature of grace dominate all of them.

Telling Parables

Dramatic revelations of grace emerge from the captivating, pregnant-with-truth stories that Jesus told. Though the dynamics of grace are more explicit in some instances than in others, a reader can dip into the parables of Jesus almost randomly and learn of grace.[30]

The initiative-taking nature of grace pervades Jesus' parable of the lost sheep (Luke 15:3-7). One lost sheep compromises a shepherd's happiness even though his ninety-nine others are accounted for and safe. Instinctively, the shepherd sets out to find the animal that is lost. Noticeably absent are grumbled denunciations from the shepherd—"That is just like a dumb sheep." "Why do sheep have to be so irresponsible?" Why the sheep is lost and whether or not the sheep deserves to be found are irrelevant issues. All that matters are finding and saving the wayward sheep. When these tasks are accomplished and the shepherd returns home accompanied by the stray member of his flock, a celebration erupts. Without understanding how much that shepherd loves all one hundred of his sheep, one cannot possibly understand the homecoming festivities.

All insights about grace are insights into the nature of God. The content of this parable illustrates this truth. God always moves first. God acts to recover and redeem the lost, no questions asked. Lostness prompts divine grace, not penitence or worthiness. People's lostness, more than goodness, commend them to God's grace.[31]

Grace deals more in what is undeserved than in what is deserved. Jesus' parable of the workers in the vineyard (Matt 20:1-15) establishes this controversial fact. In the story, each laborer receives the wages promised at the time of employment. The employer, however, decides to provide the same amount of remuneration for everybody—for those who worked only one hour as well as for those who worked all day. Cries of protest erupt. "Unfair" is the charge. Precisely! This is not a parable about fairness or even justice. It is a parable about grace (which some people deem a divine unfairness, if not a rank injustice). The employer moves beyond justice as he responds to the needs of his employees.

Grace and justice must not be confused. Justice is the assurance that every person will receive what she is due. That is the classic definition of justice—"to each his due." Grace, though, goes beyond justice. Grace offers people what they need rather than what they deserve. Grace does not ask, "What do you have coming to you?" but "What do you need?" And, grace moves to provide what is needed even before the person involved has a chance to answer that question completely.

Grace is unimpressed with both pretense about successes and honest accomplishments though always attracted to failure, lostness, and death. In his parable of the Pharisee and the tax collector (Luke 18:10-14), Jesus speaks of God's preference for spiritual emptiness over religious arrogance even if the boastfulness is supported by a detailed documentation of good deeds. Unlike most religionists (in every age), Jesus rejects the idea of justification by works and praises the justification of a person by grace alone. God can deal with broken tax collectors much better than with braggart Pharisees. What does this parable say about the moral bookkeeping that forms the foundation upon which people build their audacious discussions about who is and who is not righteous?

At times, grace seems contradictory to good sense. People who should be condemned and rejected receive affirmation and acceptance. Obviously appropriate behavior gets set aside by loving actions that are every bit as questionable as they are lavishly extravagant. In Jesus' story about a loving father and his two troublesome sons (Luke 15:11-32), the sins of the prodigal son did not stop the waiting father from greeting him with love, treating him with grace, and showering him with gifts. A simple statement of forgiveness from the father would have been more than enough to let the distressed son know he was welcome back at home. After all, the young brat had not even asked for that. But the father could not be satisfied apart from the bestowal of symbols of acceptance on his recently returned son and a festive celebration of restoration.

In reality, the resentment of the elder brother in this popular story from Jesus represents many people's attitude toward wrong-doers. A preoccupation with law, judgment, and guilt is preferable to any expression of grace. Some folks seem to fear that someone might get away with an act like one for which they had to pay dearly.

Most individuals want grace for themselves regardless of their situation. Why, then, do so many people find more delight in inflicting punishment than in extending grace when others sin?

Laughter resounds throughout the parables of Jesus. Joy and festivity regularly accompany grace. Frequently, Jesus compares entering the kingdom of God with going to a really-fun party.

Hilarious grace is unmistakable in Jesus' tale of the great banquet (Luke 14:12-24). Right off, Jesus takes another slap at religious bookkeeping. He indicates that a host should not invite to his party only guests who, in the past, have earned acceptance and who, in the future, will be sure to reciprocate the kindness. Jesus praises a person who throws a party and surrounds himself with people who have nothing to give to it but everything to gain from it—people who are poor, lame, blind, or in some other manner unacceptable. The very sight of the party goers is enough to make one howl with laughter, if not scowl with disgust. What a crummy looking crowd!

Whether kneeling on a prayer rail or bending over a pigs' trough, entering the temple or sitting in a banquet hall, a person of grace maintains a preference for losers, failures, and outcasts—"the untouchable, the unpardonable, and the unacceptable."[32] Grace does the unexpected. Grace loves the unlovable. Grace accepts in joy even those individuals who deserve no company and expect no happiness. Capon's analysis of Jesus' stories is sound, "Grace . . . is shown as a crazy initiative, a radical discontinuity because God has decided, apparently, that history cannot be salvaged even by its best continuities."[33]

Relating to Persons

Jesus ran with the wrong crowd. At least, that was the judgment of members of the religious establishment in his day. They labeled Jesus a "friend of sinners" (Matt 11:19). Those who leveled this charge at him intended it as a criticism. Jesus, however, seemed to accept it as a compliment, a commendation, perhaps a confirmation that he was doing the right thing. Grace is most concerned with those people with the most needs. In the middle of such folks is where Jesus—the Incarnation of grace—belonged.

Jesus' interpersonal relationships reeked with grace. Repeatedly, the Messiah sought out persons not because of the good they could do for him (a contact in the highest realm of government, a mover and shaker who could open almost any door into the power structure of Jerusalem, a popular personality whose affirmation of Jesus' ministry would be an influential testimony, a deep-pocketed financier who could alleviate all fiscal anxieties) but because of the good he could do for them. Jesus spent the most of his time with the very kinds of people to whom the vast majority of his peers did not offer a second glance (much less a second chance)—individuals with crippled legs, persons with abnormal arms or withered hands, folks who could not see, people with disgusting diseases. Jesus sought out individuals plagued by emotional disturbances, social ostracism, communal charges of wrongdoing, bad reputations and damaged egos. When he found such people, at his initiative Jesus gave them health, wholeness, and a start on a totally new life. Grace!

Jesus quickly grew impatient with people enamored by thoughts of self-sufficiency and illusions of self-righteousness. He had little time to give to those who saw themselves beyond grace—adept enough at good works to merit salvation apart from grace, too protective of goodness to extend grace to moral failures. Jesus evidenced a great deal more hostility toward persons meting out condemnation than to those being condemned for wrong deeds. Once, in a statement that provoked the wrath of the entire religious establishment, Jesus told a group of religious leaders, "Tax collectors and the harlots go into the kingdom of God before you" (Matt 21:31). Gasp! Grace is for the undeserving.

Adjectives did not impress Jesus. Needs, however, never failed to capture his attention. Jesus disregarded all qualifying labels such as poor, evil, wealthy, important, dangerous, questionable, ignorant, common, and religious. He saw only persons, persons in need of different kinds of attention.

For any perceptive observer, a quick study of the twelve men whom Jesus called as his disciples is a tip off regarding his propensity to act with grace. Nothing commended any one of these men to Jesus. To the contrary, if the twelve had been required to undergo psychological analyses, to supply recommendations from impressive professionals, to state their religious beliefs in terms of a creedal orthodoxy, and to pass a battery of culturally-conditioned tests to qualify for their new work, likely none would have made it. From the inception of his ministry to its conclusion, Jesus gave himself lovingly to outsiders, failures, and the irreligious.

Zacchaeus represents the mass of individuals touched by Jesus' grace. For no "good reason," only because of the graceful compassion of Christ, Zacchaeus and others were gifted with a dismissal of their pasts and with new opportunities for their futures. In every situation, Jesus seemed propelled toward persons up a tree, in a ditch, and between a rock and a hard place. On almost every occasion, the people around Jesus included beggars and prostitutes, both individuals with diseased bodies and demented personalities, failures and criminals, persons characterized by alienation and lostness. These are the people (in any age) for whom grace exists.

Responding to Institutions

Religious institutions have a dangerous, timeless tendency to cease serving as conduits of grace and to begin functioning as barriers to grace. Keeping a law can become more important than helping a person. Building up an organization of religion can take precedence over serving God and ministering to hurting people through that organization. Celebrating a festival can become more significant than living out the meaning of the event that the festival is intended to preserve. Maintaining an institution of religion can supersede meeting the needs that the institution originally was established to meet.

Jesus elevated expressions of compassion over obedience to religious legislation. He challenged entrenched traditions of morality in order to minister to a hurting personality. Jesus did not hesitate to use "sacred objects" (untouchable in the minds of many) for "secular purposes" (the judgment of his opponents) in the meeting of human needs. Jesus left no doubt that even the highest offices of civil governments have no authority that can repress the works of grace.

Any institution of religion that has become a hindrance to the distribution of grace deserves to be dismantled. Always, to the dismay of many individuals, Jesus spoke of the law serving people not vice versa. He commended delaying an experience of corporate worship in order to reconcile an estranged relationship. Despite loud protests to the contrary and harsh criticisms, Jesus spoke of tearing down the temple and raising up a new construction of grace. Jesus saw religious institutions as means to be utilized in the ministry of grace, not as ends in themselves to be served at the expense of grace.

Discussing Redemption

After Paul became a Christian (the Damascus Road experience was a dramatic episode of grace in itself), he took on the responsibility of writing about the grace so evident in the life of Jesus and interpreting its meaning for the lives of others. Like Jesus, Paul left a rich legacy of understanding regarding grace that goes far beyond comments in which the actual word appears. Passages from Paul such as Romans 8 and 2 Corinthians 5:19-21 comprise invaluable expositions on grace though the term "grace" cannot be found anywhere in them.

Central in the thought of Paul is the Incarnation of Christ—a grace-event in every sense. Though Paul does not use the word "grace" in his great hymn on the Incarnation in Philippians 2:5-11, that text is a wonderful exposition on grace. Integral to the nature of grace are self-emptying actions, humble identification with need, and compassionate service even at a cost of death. All followers of Christ are expected (commissioned) to serve as incarnations of grace—"Have this mind among yourselves, which is yours in Christ Jesus."

18.
The Very Idea!

Dostoyevski once observed that love in practice is a harsh and terrible thing compared with love in dreams. A similar comment can be made regarding the nature of grace as exercised in personal experience *vis á vis* grace acclaimed as a soteriological doctrine. Understood on the basis of insights from the Bible, grace is radical.

Grace runs against the grain of human experience, breaks with traditions, defies reason, and frequently looks just plain foolish. Grace takes people where they would not go naturally and involves them in the initiation of actions that whey would just as soon avoid. Grace brings about strange fellowships that may cause bystanders to raise their eyebrows or to turn their heads. Often grace requires getting dirty, risking the acquisition of a bad name, and being misunderstood.

To live by grace is to experience salvation. But that is only the beginning. Look at what it means to live by grace: to place love above the law and individuals over institutions, to offer help when it is needed whether or not it is deserved or requested, to grant forgiveness even before a penitent confession, to cease judging people and to be ceaseless in encouraging people, to find delight in ministry and to see the acceptance of failures as a reason for festivity, and to know that the joy of salvation is even more full when shared than when found.

Grace is God's gift to the undeserving. Grace is a gift that once received must be shared. Grace reaches out for persons plagued by lostness, loneliness, failures, and illness. The very idea.

Grace! The very idea!

V.
What about Judgment and Punishment?

"It was a terrible sin," she continued, "really it was. . . . I acted like a foolish adolescent. My state of mind was no excuse. I deserved to be punished. So what did God do? He sent . . . a reward instead of a punishment. Does that make any sense at all? Can I love the result and still repent the sin?"

Andrew M. Greeley
An Occasion of Sin

"When push comes to shove, you want a nasty-nice little judge who will keep crimes against faith off the streets. But God won't even do that.
. . . Unfaith is its own punishment. All God ever does is confirm the stupid sentence of alienation it pronounces on itself; all he ever condemns are people who want to be more respectable than he is."

Robert Farrar Capon
Parables of Judgment

"But what about judgment and punishment?" No sooner is that question asked (usually with impatience, if not defiance and panic), than a frequently present, always fascinating though often silent, aspect of the human spirit is revealed. Too much talk about grace sets some people on edge. They do not seem to want the truth of the gospel to be that good, that liberating, and that joyful. So, they quickly turn their attention to judgment and punishment, which (from their point of view) are more understandable, predictable, and (in their opinion) "fair." Such people find discussions centered on retaliation, condemnation, and sinners "getting what they deserve" more palatable than conversations about compassion, grace, and forgiveness. They fear the implicit suggestion that sinners may go "scot free."

Why? Why do people prefer to talk about judgment and punishment? Several possible explanations exist.

Perhaps intellectual integrity produces the interest. Maybe it is a genuine philosophical or theological concern. Thinking people with a desire for understanding want to know how to reconcile compassion and wrath, guilt and grace, judgment and hope in relation to God.

Sometimes, though, an overriding interest in judgment and punishment springs from a person's own involvement in a hurtful situation and/or battle with disturbed emotions. "Surely, there is some reason for all of this mess," an individual muses, "So many pained persons and a society filled with chaotic conditions must be products of divine punishment."

More negatively, a quizzical fascination with punishment can signal the thought of an agnostic. Reading about grace and mistakenly sensing that people do not have to bear the consequences of wrong-doing, a skeptic concludes that God has been caught with a divine hand in the cookie jar. Sensing that at long last a flaw in the deity has been discovered, a question about judgment is hurled to the heavens. Enlightenment is not the goal of this exercise, but rather an attempt to cause embarrassment for God. The questioner imagines leveling an unanswerable charge against God.

Saddest among the sources of judgment-and-punishment-related questions are persons who view God as a "holy terror" rather than perfect love. These folks understand Christianity more as a compliance with certain words than as obedience to grace. They follow Jesus as a stormtrooper type of Savior who snatches people from Hell rather than as a servant-oriented redeemer who makes possible a quality of life that seems like heaven on earth. Such people approach all of life from a perspective of threats and fears rather than promises and faith. Often individuals like this are quick to point out that they have suffered for their sins and want everybody else to share that same fate. They feel that living as good people has required pain and difficulties for them. Thus, they do not want anyone unwilling to pay the price for righteousness to enjoy a bargain related to sin. To people with this mentality, love and grace look like weaknesses. They actually favor an accounts-keeping, flames-breathing God who roams the earth making people suffer for every moral snafu.

Regardless of the specific motivation behind it, the question about divine judgment and punishment is worthy of both serious consideration and a careful response. An affirmation of the primacy of grace need not fear wrestling with this inquiry.

19.
Judgment: Yes and No

Whether or not people are subjects of judgment is hardly debatable from a biblical perspective. Judgment is a reality (Rom 14:10b). Crucial to an accurate understanding of judgment, though, are the definition of its nature and the identification of the judge.

God is identified as a judge throughout the Bible. In the Old Testament, God's judgment is primarily, though not exclusively, informed by the law. From a judicial perspective, laws or commandments give meaning to the concept of justice and become the criteria by which justice is measured. When the law of God was violated (corporately as well as individually), negative judgments from God could be expected. God's judgments differ from human judgments, however, even in the narratives of the Old Testament. Occasionally, God extended forgiveness when it was totally undeserved, thus catching everyone by surprise. God's love and mercy supersede the dictates of law, transcend the requirements of justice.[34]

In the New Testament, judgment ceases to be a legal matter. At the center of divine concern are people's reception of grace and actions of grace. Divine judgment remains a reality. But now the basis of judgment is a person's relationship with Jesus (the incarnation of grace) and ministry to and through Jesus (deeds of compassionate grace).

Though no one is guiltless before God, everyone is acceptable to God. Negative judgments and ultimately separation from God always result from human choices, never from the divine will. God desires condemnation for no one. God seeks reconciliation and fellowship with everyone. God, however, respects an individual's exercise of her divinely-given freedom. Thus, if a person freely chooses to live apart from grace, God goes along with that decision. Note though, negative judgment has its source in a person exercising his free will negatively. We judge ourselves.[35] God simply confirms the judgments people make.

Judgment is a reality. God is a judge. Compassion and grace are the basic criteria by which God exercises judgment. Jesus serves as an agent of God's judgment. All of that is certain.

Equally certain is the truth that no one other than God should pass judgment on a person. Old Testament writers condemned people who set themselves up as judges over others.[36] In the New Testament, Jesus left no doubt regarding the divine demand that no individual seek to pass judgment on another person. Great damage accompanies a failure to heed this declaration from Jesus.

Jesus calls upon his followers to serve as agents of grace, not as dispensers of judgment. No human being has either the capacity or the responsibility to pass judgment on another person. God commands people to heed, herald, and implement grace, not to level judgment. To disregard that divine charge and act as a judge in relation to anyone is to assume the role of God (an obscene sacrilege on earth and in heaven) and to indicate a desire to live apart from grace (a foolish, hell-bent decision).

People's passion for passing judgments on each other constitutes one of the major barriers to the implementation of grace individually and to the formation of a community of grace corporately. For that reason, special attention must be given both to the number and to the nature of the New Testament's prohibitions about one person judging another person.

Jesus spoke with simplicity and clarity on this matter. All that he said can be reduced to three words: "Do not judge." The author of the Fourth Gospel devotes special attention to Jesus' observations about the inability of individuals to judge each other. People tend to express judgments based upon appearances (John 7:24) and human standards (John 8:13). Both of these bases of judgment are unacceptable to the God of grace who always looks beneath the surface of a person's life and seeks to convey mercy to all people.

In the synoptic Gospels, Jesus' words about judgment combine prohibition and warning. People are told to refrain from making judgments about each other. Also, they are advised that if they insist on relating to other people with judgment rather than grace, they will thereby establish the criterion by which God relates to them (Matt 7:1; Luke 6:37). What a terrifying thought! Individuals receive from God what they give to each other—judgment or grace.

Spiritual maturity and good motivations aside, it seems that after reading Jesus' words of warning about passing judgment on others, a person would prefer to live by grace rather than by judgment as a matter of sheer self-interest. Who wants to be judged constantly (perhaps harshly and wrongly as well), when being bathed in grace is a possibility? What kind of person would want to continue dispatching negative judgments on other people after being told by Jesus that "the measure (of judgment) you give will be the measure you get" (Matt 7:1)? Who honestly can pray the model prayer from Jesus apart from a great deal of fear—asking that God forgive us as (in the same manner) we forgive other people? Frankly, I do not want my practice of forgiveness to serve as the model by which God grants forgiveness to me!

How strange that many individuals prefer the image of a courtroom to that of a mercy seat when thinking about God. No one can have it both ways. Apparently, some folks want to relate to other people in judgment and then turn to God seeking grace for themselves. Impossible! Everybody decides individually whether to live by judgment or by grace. What is meted out to others is in turn received from others and from God. Why is there not a massively-supported urgent push to get on with the establishment of fellowships of mercy?

Jesus' strong prohibition against persons passing judgment on each other sounded so clearly in the Gospels resounds with remarkable frequency throughout the rest of the New Testament. In the small tract on practical Christianity known as James, an echo of Jesus' statements about judgment appears followed by a question intended to expose the audacity of a self-appointed judge—"So who, then, are you to judge your neighbor?" (Ja 4:12) No sooner does the author of 1 Peter mention judgment than he urges his readers to be "good stewards of the manifold grace of God" (1 Pet 4:10).

Paul's letters reveal an almost defiant defensiveness about judgment on the part of the apostle. Obviously, the man from Tarsus was the target of many people's negative judgments. He makes light of the influence of such judgments (1 Cor 4:3) and counsels his colleagues in the faith to not allow their spiritual practices to be affected by the judgments of others (Col 3:16). Paul readily recognizes the judgment of the Lord (1 Cor 11:31), but allows no one else to assume such a position of sovereignty over his life—"Why should my liberty be subject to the judgment of someone else's conscience?" (1 Cor 10:29)

Writing to the Romans, Paul succinctly states the New Testament's teachings on judgment (Rom 14:10-13). Judgment is inevitable for everybody. But each person's accountability—subjection to judgment—is oriented only to God. People—especially the people of God—are not to pass judgment on one another or others. They are not even to say anything evil about someone else. The Christ-based mission in need of attention involves the removal of all hindrances to redemption. Grace is to prevail.

Such statements of straight-forward clarity defy misunderstanding or false interpretation. What, then, is the issue? In the face of overwhelming prohibitions against such action, why do people persist in judging each other?

Maybe self-righteousness is the answer. Some people simply discount the mandates of the scriptures and see themselves as "good enough" to judge others. They act as self-appointed "defenders of all that is good." But the terrible truth is that such folks attack wrong-doers with an enthusiasm and viciousness much more akin to evil than to good. Not even God seems to defend morality and divinity like they do!

Another possible explanation for the persistence of judgment among some persons is the phenomenon in which an individual seeks to elevate himself by putting down most everyone else. Such an individual needs always to be able to point to someone in comparison with whom she is really good. Often at stake in this situation also is a "chip on the shoulder" kind of righteousness, an attitude that avows "it has cost me dearly to be as good as I am and I want everybody who is different from me to have to pay through the nose for being that way."

For whatever reasons it is done, anyone establishing himself as a judge over another person assumes a prerogative that belongs only to God. The outcome of that action today is no different from its earliest precedent in Eden. People who attempt to play God find themselves farther and farther separated from God.

God judges. The dominant image of divine judgment, however, is not that of a formal, carefully-guarded tribunal devoted to exacting justice but a wide-open, easily-accessible holy place dedicated to dispensing grace.

20.
Punishment: Source and Purpose

Sin *is* punished. God's will in relation to sinners, however, is forgiveness, not punishment. Grace dominates divine actions even in response to sins sure to set in motion serious problems.

In seeking to understand a proper reaction to sin and sinners, a look at the life of Jesus can be as unnerving as it is enlightening. Especially is this true for persons who assign punishment a high priority.

Jesus' controversial counsel about turning the other cheek and going a second mile, when confronted by evil, provides an important insight into his total way of life. More than once, Jesus indicated that the proper response to evil is good—not retaliation from the offended but compassion for the offender. What Jesus taught, he lived. Despite charges that he ignored wickedness, Jesus continued to identify with and befriend sinners, not push them away or seek to have them locked up. Finally, from the cross, Jesus prayed for the forgiveness of his executioners. In the life of Jesus, grace abounded. Love prevailed.

"But, don't beg the question," someone protests, "Does God punish sin? Answer!" In one sense, yes. People who disobey God's will experience the chill of a negative response from God. A negative reaction from God, however, always arises from a positive purpose. God, as revealed in Jesus Christ, is not an immature, childish deity who throws temper tantrums when divine love is rejected and hurls hurtful spiritual stones at people who ignore the divine will. Rather, even when cruelly spurned, God turns not toward vindictiveness but forgiveness.

Experiences commonly categorized as punishment for sins are in reality the inevitable consequences of sin. Life-negating, joy-defeating, meaning-eradicating developments inhere in sin. People who sin actually set in motion forces that are sure to result in negative consequences. Sinners bring punishment upon themselves. As Sovereign of the universe, God often gets saddled with the blame for such harmful developments. God, however, wills good rather than evil; abundant life, not a tortured life. As the author of freedom and the ultimate advocate of free will, God allows people not only to make decisions about right and wrong, good and evil, but to live with the consequences of the decisions they make.

Certain choices and actions among human beings will always be accompanied by negative consequences—whether dubbed as "punishments" or tagged with some other name. A person who places hope in false gods can count on experiencing a lack of fulfillment, an abundance of frustration, and the depths of despair. People who seek to settle disputes by violent means are doomed to know both physical and emotional pain. A decision to violate a covenant relationship sets in motion distrust, insecurity, and chaos (internally and externally). Promiscuous sexual activities bring about a diminished sense of self-worth, erode a capacity for fulfilling fidelity, and hurt the individuals involved emotionally and spiritually (and sometimes physically). God wills none of that. The so-called "punishment" for such evil deeds is inherent in the deeds. Sin carries within it the seeds of destruction.

"Well," a follow up question is on the way, "If God is so big on grace and the all-powerful ruler of the universe, why doesn't God prevent sinners from experiencing any negative consequences for their sins?" Nowhere in the revelation of God in the Bible is punishment praised as an end in itself. What some people dub as punishment also can be understood as a divine push toward redemption. God works in all things for good—for redemption. Love acts to correct wrongdoing in the life of the one loved rather than allow it to persist unchallenged.

In terms of sheer potential, God could eradicate the predictable consequences of sin, thus allowing hope in idolatry, joy amid infidelity, and trust in the face of lost integrity. But, what kind of God would do this? The issue is not the potential of God but the nature of God. God is love. God is grace. God wills that the crises, troubles, and problems that result from sin lead to positive changes in life. Then, the joy that accompanies repentance and forgiveness will overshadow lingering pain. The decision to live by grace will reduce the entirety of the difficult past to no more than a bad memory.

"What about Hell?" That question is as predictable as the one that follows it: "Is Hell even a possibility given God's propensity toward grace?" The answer is "Yes. Yes, Hell is a reality as well as a possibility." But that positive answer is never a source of pleasure, a response voiced with satisfaction or delight.

No helpful way exists to think about concepts such as Hell and Heaven except by means of imagery. Thus, recall the parable in which Jesus speaks of a prodigal son, a loving-forgiving father, and a resentful, non-merciful elder brother. Where grace abounds, life takes on the nature of a party. Sinners are robed and fed, not rebuffed and dismissed. Forgiveness, restoration, and mercy prevail, and each evokes an incredible joy. If a person, like the elder brother in Jesus' story, cannot accept that—if one, anyone, prefers rejection to acceptance, retaliation to compassion, and vindictiveness to forgiveness—then the party—the only party worth attending—is forever out of reach for that person. Devoid of a positive response to the grace of God and empty of any trace of grace for others, a person has no alternative but to turn away from the sounds of music, laughter, and fellowship; to walk away from the festival of love; to reject an invitation to the banquet of redemption. That is Hell! And what's more, the Hell of Hell is that all who experience it know they still are loved by the God throwing the party and, more than anything else on earth or in heaven, God wants them right there in the middle of all of the hilarity having the time of their lives, but they chose not to be a part of the party.

Nobody has to see to it that sinners are punished for their sins. Every sin has punishment enough inherent in it. Look around: A young woman dreadfully fears another relationship. A man strains with all of his might to convince his peers of the truthfulness of another lie lest his entire existence begin to come unraveled. A family is broken in spirit because of estranged relationships among its members. A panic-stricken business lady watches the rapid, downward spiral of her company's sales as a result of false advertising. A man cannot trust another human being because of his own betrayals of the trust of others. These people do not need more punishment. Why would anyone want more difficulties thrust upon such folks? They need help, redemption, refuge. God wills for all such people an experience of grace. God's people commit themselves to the task of translating that divine intention into a practical reality.

Ironically (and sadly), voicing denunciatory judgments on others (which Jesus opposed) and inflicting difficulties as a means of punishing people's sins are most commonly actions of persons waving a banner of righteousness and claiming the name of Jesus. They must ignore the fact that Jesus warned against judgment and equated true righteousness with grace.

But they persist in their self-defined mission as God's "hatchet people." This raises another question. Is a community of grace possible among those who identify themselves as "the faithful"? Yes, by all means, if the nature of the gospel is understood. If not, architects of a contemporary city of refuge will come from somewhere else.

Imagine how different life would be if all the people committed to passing judgment on wrongdoers and preoccupied with guaranteeing the infliction of appropriate amounts of punishment upon them were captivated by God's compassion and motivated to become agents of grace. The intention of "giving people hell" could be replaced by a will to work on the agenda of heaven. Condemnations that kill would be silenced. Refuge would be available for all in need of it.

Jesus embodied what the most insightful ancients had envisioned about God. In a remarkable, powerful passage from the Psalms, the writer speaks as a prophet (Ps 103:8-10). The songwriter declares that God does not "deal" with people "according to their sins" seeking to "repay us according to our iniquities" because God is "merciful and gracious, slow to anger and abounding in steadfast love." How individuals behave toward errant persons depends to a great extent on the accuracy of their understanding and the authenticity of their acceptance of this merciful God. Jesus incarnates this God.

Jesus did not seek to level penalties for evil acts or measure the revenge to be exacted because of sinful hurts. In dealing with sin, the strategy of Jesus was to accept its burden, to take upon himself—to absorb into his very being—its evil hurt, in order to extend grace and redemption to the sinner whom God loves.[37]

Frankly, many people find Jesus' position on the priority of grace obnoxious and unacceptable. Crucial, then, is the correct answer to the question of whether or not Jesus had divine authority. If he did, then a life of grace cannot be a debatable subject or a negotiable option for the people of God.

VI.
Media of Grace

"The will, the desire of the lover is simply the beloved herself in her freedom: God just wants *us*. And the calling of the beloved is simply to love: The glory and the misery of the love affair is the master image for the understanding of our vocation. . . . The will of God . . . is his longing that we will take the risk of being nothing but ourselves, desperately in love."

Robert Farrar Capon
Hunting the Divine Fox

"It's not like one chance, and if you blow it, that's that. Pretty clever of God to give us second chances, you know? Nothing ever lost till it's really lost."

"Pure grace."

"Right." She grinned crookedly. "Well, sometimes not all that pure, but still grace."

Andrew M. Greeley
All About Women

Is that all there is? No question exists about the prevalence of troubled people. At some point, most everybody wants to run from life or for life? Little debate is offered regarding the centrality of grace within Christianity. But, is that all there is—a recognition of human needs and an affirmation of divine grace? Can the two ever be brought together— grace-needful people and the grace-full gospel? What about a giving up place? Apart from addressing the question of whether or not a refuge is probable, is the persistent and practical demonstration of grace by a community even possible?

Unfortunately, most persons do not think much about the importance of grace until they find themselves in need of it. As long as life is going well, or at least as long as a positive front can be maintained, grace receives little attention. Individuals pledge their allegiance to fairness and justice, insisting that sinners and other failures get what they deserve. A few folks may even have the audacity to belittle those in trouble by way of self comparisons: "I have been tempted, but I rejected temptation." "I could have messed up many times, but I worked hard to succeed. It could be the same for you if you had really tried." But when life caves in for such people (regardless of who or what causes the avalanche), grace quickly surfaces as a high priority item for them.

Though disturbing, that tendency is not surprising. In the New Testament, the people most cognizant of the significance of grace and most receptive to a ministry of grace were those for whom nothing else was available. The same is true today. Grace is recognized most clearly and affirmed most readily when a person's situation in life is most desperate. In fact, until a person experiences a need for grace, the pro- found importance of grace may be missed.

Of course, everyone needs grace. All that is in question is the matter of timing. When will a recognition of the need for grace be realized and admitted?

Thankfully, God's grace is always available. Whenever a person confesses a need for grace, the gift of grace is already present. No one has to face a day devoid of divine grace at any time.

But the availability of a community of grace is another matter. Not by a long shot do all the people who need the ministry of a community of grace receive such help at the time of their greatest need. Reasons are no mystery. Too few persons have faced into their own needs realistically. Not enough individuals have humbly committed themselves to serve as agents of the divine grace of which they are beneficiaries.

So, honestly, what about the possibility of a community of grace? That question emerged during a quiet dinner conversation with a caring friend who is a priest in need of care. Shaking his head in a negative response to the inquiry, my friend said softly, "I just don't know. I am not sure you can ever expect grace except on an individual basis. Communities may not be capable of grace."

Predictably, anti-institutionalists decry the possibility of a community of grace. Their protest rests on a conviction that all institutions are evil. No exceptions. Thus, the very idea of a grace-filled institution is out of the question for them.

For most of my adult life, I have steadfastly refused to accept such pessimism. I must admit, though, at times I wonder if my resistance has been the result of naivete, wishful thinking, idealism, or just plain stubbornness.

Strong arguments support the possibility of a community of grace. Jesus called his disciples to demonstrate God-like initiatives in their lives—overcoming evil with good, helping the helpless, caring for the undeserving, and extending forgiveness without limits. Social structures responsive to people in need are a part of the divine will for life in the world as revealed in the Bible. Surely God would not commission people to the pursuit of an impossibility.

Biblically-informed scholars take the matter a step further. Daniel Day Williams says flatly, "It is false to assume that grace works only in the individual."[38] God's grace is mediated through God's people—individually and corporately. David Baily Harned agrees, citing his belief that grace creates and develops a community between people just as grace forms a community between people and God.[39]

To be sure, reticence about grace appears among unexpected people and in surprising places. A minister's phone call regarding a mutual friend who is in trouble severely disappointed me. From the other end of the line came these words: "Please understand that I am all for understanding, forgiveness, and all of that. But, there are political realities to be considered. The man is identified with us and what is being said about him could hurt us. He has got to go. We must find a way to get him out of his present position."

My letter of recommendation for a friend in need of employment was addressed to an acquaintance who is an expert on biblical teachings about grace. His written response left me down-hearted. "Indiscretions in this man's life make it impossible for me to consider him for a position. Maybe we are using a double standard of judgment in his case. Call it what you will, that is the position of this Christian institution."

A religious bureaucrat voiced all the "right words" when I spoke with him about a member of his church who needed help. With a precision sharpened (or dulled, depending on one's point of view) by well-practiced clichés, he delivered a lunch-table lecture about exercising bad judgment, taking responsibility for wrongdoing, and the availability of forgiveness if the person displayed sincere and sorrowful penitence. When he finished his professional presentation, I asked the minister what he personally was willing to do to assist this man. His well-rehearsed discourse gave way to an awkward silence. Finally, in a very pious tone of voice, the pastor said, "I would like to think we (I don't know the constituency of the "we"—surely it was not "he and God") could be redemptive."

"Good God!"—the thought raced through my mind, though the words did not cross my lips. "You would like to *think* you, we, or whoever could be redemptive!" If redemption is up for grabs, a negotiable option dependent upon the quality of a sinner's public confessions to some pastor with illusions of an elevated personal position, what is distinctive about Christianity? If grace is not available from one who identifies himself as a proclaimer of the gospel of grace, how believable is the gospel?

Despite an abundance of evidence to dispute the validity of my assertion, grace is available. Yes, the grace of God. But more. The grace of God is mediated through the people of God. A community of grace is possible. God's will for the establishment and empowerment of such a community is a matter of revelation.

Granted, the human factor in this equation is cause for concern. A complete implementation of the divine will is in question. Will the people of God dare to serve as media of the grace of God?

21.
Dispelling Myths

Myths mess up community and short circuit ministry. Especially when grace is involved—grace as the foundation for community and the motivation behind ministry. Myths can outright prevent, as well as make difficult, the implementation of grace. Thus, dispelling myths by telling the truth is a crucial work of grace.

Numerous grace-less untruths have been talked about loudly enough and gone unchallenged long enough that scores of persons have uncritically accepted them as solid ideas that justify inaction in the face of need. The sad result is the persistence of a type of thinking that is problematic for the development of grace-based fellowships. Before giving further attention to the formation of a community of grace, what has been learned about the gift of grace needs to be brought to bear on these well-entrenched lies.

At issue here is a conflict between grace-filled truths and disgraceful myths. "Disgrace," a term coined by David Seamands, denotes that which works in direct opposition to grace. Grace is constructive, encouraging, and growth-inducing. Disgrace is destructive, stunting, perverting, and thus life-impairing.[40] Disgraceful myths must die so grace can get on with its redemptive work.

Myths about People

Damaging myths about people erect imposing barriers to expressions of grace. The problem is not a carefully-thought-out philosophy of human development in which analytical reasoning has established specific methods for dealing with both good and evil in a manner that improves the quality of life for everyone. Not at all. At stake are ill-thought-out (if examined at all), detrimental ideas that often are verbalized only in colloquial asides or by way of throw-away comments intended to "write off" certain individuals.

Either in a snap judgment or by way of a more hardened prediction, during their lunch time conversation, two business colleagues speak about a man in trouble: *"He is finished!"* Or, at the monthly meeting of the neighborhood garden club, when the name of an absent member is mentioned, the consensus of those present is that *"She is ruined for life."*

Can such estimates be sustained in light of the gospel? No. In fact, the response of the gospel to any declaration of a person's irreversible demise is "Never!" As long as the grace of God has not been ultimately rejected, no one is ever totally ruined or completely finished.

Of course, negative consequences inhere in certain acts of behavior. Damage may be sustained vocationally or familially. Emotions may be disturbed or good health threatened. Trust may be eroded and confidence shaken. But, none of this has to be terminal in any sense. Central to the gospel is the possibility of new beginnings, the creation of a future even when tomorrow seems in doubt.

Grace functions most dramatically amid the debris of devastated lives. That is where grace belongs. That is what grace is for. According to the Gospels, brokenness, hurt, defeat, and failure are the conditions to which grace is most responsive. Those who know grace best are people who have learned about grace during the worst moments of their lives.

Human judgments about dead ends for persons fail to take into account the re-creative possibilities of God's grace. Many people have served God and others most mercifully after their involvement in experiences that appeared to be life-destroying. Usually, the pattern is far from neat—one bad experience followed by a change for the better and then constant good. All too often, the graph of a person's development includes sharply rising and falling lines zigzagging all across a chart. Disruptive episodes intersect and disrupt periods of progress. God is in both. God is accustomed to bringing the best out of the worst, good out of evil. Even death can be swept away mercifully by means of a divinely-breathed resurrection. Just when some people judge everything to be ending, grace pushes problem-laden persons until they are poised on the edge of a new beginning.

In his profoundly insightful book *The Wounded Healer,* Henri Nouwen reflects on this spiritual truth so apparent in the Bible.[41] Wounds often provide the most impeccable credentials for persons interested in service as healers. Obviously, no right-thinking person would deliberately set out to fail, to suffer tragedy, to cause life to cave in on her merely as a preparation for beneficent actions. When addressed by grace, however, marks of devastation do become invaluable in the cause of redemption.

Grace's counsel for problem-plagued people regarding their increased potential for service is not just a psychological ploy intended to make them feel better. To interpret an individual's tragedy from the perspective of grace, pointing out new possibilities for meaningful ministry, is not merely to do the person a favor, to extend kindness. These grace-addressed people are needed in the ongoing service of grace. Who better can speak of how life can come from death or demonstrate how unparalleled sensitivity and helpfulness can emerge from incredible hurt?

A community of grace affirms and facilitates new beginnings for all people. At the very point when an individual is judged to be "finished," advocates of grace assert, "Not so." With a recognition that life beyond tragedy may even be of a better quality, grace-full people say to each other, "Let's give her a fourth opportunity" and declare to the troubled person, "It is time to begin again. We are with you. Live under the mercy."

Another combination of remarks representative of disgrace is the all-too-frequent conclusion of persons not wishing to be bothered by anyone who appears to present problems in need of attention. Conversations about a young man who repeatedly has been in and out of trouble invariably cause someone to declare, *"We might as well give up on him."* A difficulty-ridden family is made the brunt of harsh judgment as narrow-sighted observers decide, *"They are just not worth any more of our efforts to help."* Such comments may be understandable from the perspective of impatience and fatigue among people who have seen their efforts to help others swallowed up in frustration. But these kinds of negative estimates of persons are abominable myths from the point of view of grace.

Worth is absolutely an irrelevant concern for grace. Were that not the case, if merit actually mattered, something other than grace would be involved. By definition, grace is an initiative for good aimed at the undeserving. Only in this way, by grace, has anyone ever been reconciled with God. Think about it carefully. No one really deserves a redemptive relationship with the Holy Creator-Redeemer. Any thought of earning such a divine-human experience is completely ludicrous. God's grace comes as sheer gift. Always. Likewise, grace, if exercised at all, is always exercised as a gift within the human community.

From the standpoint of the gospel, no one can ever do anything (once or repeatedly) that places him outside the realm of grace. The crucial issue is never the devaluation of an individual, but the relentless, indefatigable, constantly-bent-toward-love redemptive activity of God. Any true community of God's people works unceasingly at re-creation for everyone.

In reality, most people give up on themselves as well as on others long before God does. God *never* gives up on a person. God is motivated not by who people are or by what people do but by the essence of the divine nature that is grace. The Israelites repeatedly rebelled against God's will—in Egypt, in the wilderness, and in the promised land. But God mercifully made possible their exodus from Egypt, provided manna for them in the wilderness, and gave them covenanted guidance once they were settled. Similarly, Jesus, the incarnation of grace, ministered to those who mistreated him and provided redemption for those who killed him. What if God had given up on Abraham, Moses, or David? What if Jesus had decided that Peter, James, and John were not worth his efforts? God never quits offering the gift of grace to anyone.

A community of grace images God's persistent mercy. No one is excluded from grace or from the grace community for any reason. God deemed every individual important enough to redeem even at a cost of the ignoble death of Jesus. Surely, then, every person is important enough to God's people to justify endless efforts to convey grace to her.

Occasionally self-appointed critics say of disparaged acquaintances: *"She is beyond redemption"* or *"He has fallen from grace."* Pure myths!

No person is so evil as to stand outside of God's love and beyond the reach of divine redemption. In fact, the depth and breadth of God's love are never any clearer than when viewed in relation to a sinner. Jesus stated publicly that his mission was to reach the despised, the dejected, and the damned; the downcast and the outcast ("Those who are well have no need of a physician, but those who are sick. . . . I came not to call the righteous, but sinners." Matt 9:12-13). Paul captured the truth in a succinct, powerful statement: "God shows his love for us in that *while we were yet sinners* Christ died for us" (Rom 5:8).

The very idea of falling from grace fails to stand up to severe questioning. The omnipresent God is ever-present grace. Persons can no more get away from God's grace than they can escape God's presence. The Psalmist contemplated this truth beneficially, confessing to God, "Thou art there!" whether speculating on life in heaven or Sheol, on land or sea, in darkness or in light (Ps 139:7-12). Retaining the imagery of the myth, if a person falls from grace, he falls into grace.

Any suggestion that a person may be beyond grace and redemption reveals an inadequate comprehension of the nature of God. Francis Thompson conveys this truth beautifully in the imagery of her infamous poem "The Hound of Heaven." God sniffs out and goes after people in need. God tracks down even those people who are insanely trying to get away. To suspect God's inability to salvage an individual is to contemplate a god who is way too small, not the God revealed in the Bible and fleshed-out in Jesus.

A community of God's people reflects the Divine's relentless search for all persons in need of redemption. Not every one may accept the opportunity to experience grace, but all must be pursued until confronted with that choice.

Myths about Grace

To be praised so highly as the divinely provided basis of salvation, grace sure takes an abusive pounding when people talk of its role in interpersonal relations. Sometimes it seems as if grace is considered a one-time opportunity provided so people can "get right with God." For that purpose, grace deserves great acclaim. After that, however, grace recedes in its importance and merit for attention. People are expected to get with the religious program, at least to give the appearance of a capacity for perfection, and to live with the judgmental wrath and other negative consequences produced by whatever wrongdoings occur. One experience of grace is enough for anyone.

Wrong! This is the response of the biblical message to this ill-conceived view of grace that distorts the nature of God. The God revealed in Jesus of Nazareth is not a divinity who dangles grace in front of people to win their allegiance and then suddenly withdraws it once they are committed to the divine will. No one has to worry about grace as a now-you-see-it-now-you-don't truth. Mercy is not a possession of God; it is the very nature of God.[42]

"Grace is for weaklings," snorts a macho-minded religionist. He continues, "God must be fed up with all our talk about compassion. Read the Old Testament. God doesn't let people get away with their sins. God authors devastation like that at Babel, Sodom, and Gomorrah or rains fire as on Mount Carmel. People who talk so much about grace are

fainthearted liberals with stomachs too weak to tolerate the rough and tumble work of judgment."

A correct understanding of strength is crucial to seeing the fallacy of this myth. This is not easily accomplished though. Radical differences exist between biblical teachings and cultural expectations related to weakness and strength. Often popular perception labels as stark weakness the very actions that Jesus praised as indications of strength. And, the apostle Paul is the source of more confusion than help on this subject. He confessed that he was strongest when he was weak and weakest when he was strong.

Conflicting attitudes about strength and weakness dot the Gospel documents. The issue is caught up in recurring questions that must be answered. Which is most indicative of true strength: reconciliation or retribution, turning the other cheek when hit by someone or going for the jugular in the other person, forgiving or getting even, praying for enemies or attacking them, bearing the burdens of others or ignoring them, judging evil or seeking to affect redemption? Jesus answers those inquiries by way of his actions.

Little or no willpower or strength is required to jump on the band-wagon of condemnation for an individual whose sins have been publicly disclosed. Anybody can pass along rumors that ruin the reputation of a person suspected of an evil deed. That requires no strength! All kinds of people pontificate about how wrong-doing cannot be tolerated. How much courage does that take? Who cannot toss into the social garbage dump people whom it would be costly to help? What is admirable about folks who punish everyone by the letter of the law? Weaklings!

To see strength, take a long look at people standing with a condemned person, pleading for sensitive understanding in response to moral failures, and speaking up for forgiveness. To view power, watch individuals willfully accepting the brunt of anger understandably directed at someone else and helping people whom others like to hurt. That is strength according to Jesus. Grace is strong.

All debates about grace, strength, and weakness can be enlightened by the person and ministry of Jesus—the epitome of grace with no equals, a matchless tower of strength.

Maybe the most problematic myth about grace is the assumption: *"Grace conveys a permissiveness that contributes to immorality."* Innumerable clichés cluster about these comments: "We must not be soft on sin." "People should get what they deserve." "Judgment is all that people understand, thus the only response to evil that will stop evil." Immediately obvious in these declarations are a misperception of the nature of judgment, an over-simplification of the issue of merit, and a gross misunderstanding of the nature of grace.

By no stretch of the imagination is grace soft on sin. Grace hates Christ-killing evil. Grace does require, however, that efforts aimed at the redemption of sinners accompany all condemnations of their sins.

Communiques of grace do not indicate or create permissiveness for immorality. Righteousness is grace's interest. But, grace deems it more effective to move people toward righteousness by love, support, forgiveness, and encouragement than by barbs, denouncements, and depersonalizing put-downs. Graciousness, not permissiveness, is the commendation of grace because righteousness is best understood not as the absence of sin but as the presence of grace.

Myths about Graceful Ministry

Bringing grace to bear on hurting people is never easy. Two popular myths have been spawned to justify a lack of involvement in such risky ministry. Both do spiritual damage to their perpetrators rather than help them.

A frequently heard comment among people who have been "burned" —taken advantage of and hurt—is, *"It is dangerous to care too much about anyone."* In conversations among jilted lovers, individuals who have been through divorces, and persons who have had their trust in someone shattered, at least one person (and usually more) will say, *"I will never again allow myself to love anyone that much."*

Such a resolve is closely akin to the basic intention of ancient Stoic philosophers. They praised reason and scorned passions. These astute thinkers sought to avoid anything they could not control, emotions included, concluding that if they had no feelings, they would know no hurt. The logic seems impressive. An exercise of careful logic, however, is no guarantee of a meaningful life.

A shutdown of emotions produces individuals more like wooden planks than vibrant persons. No one can steel her emotions selectively. Efforts to eradicate a capacity to hurt also erode possibilities for happiness. Laughter and tears come from the same place.

Just prior to writing these thoughts, I took a phone call from an obviously troubled woman requesting time for a conversation. When I inquired about her need, she told me she could no longer weep. As we talked on, she spoke of her lack of joy as well. She saw no connection between the two.

At this very point, wisdom begins to emerge from several New Testament passages that previously may have seemed like indecipherable double-talk. Life knows no greater moments than those caught up in expressions of love. Jesus said that the singular most profound demonstration of love is the gift of life for a friend. Thus, life really is gained by losing it. Only in giving does a person discover anything worth receiving. Apart from understanding the nature and necessity of a gift, a person misses the meaning and ministry of grace.

To those who buy into the myth about the danger of caring too much, proponents of grace declare the truth of a far greater danger: not caring enough.

Honesty among persons is required for community among them to be realized. Falsehoods damage and finally, if unchecked, destroy fellowship. Myths about grace and its relationship to persons are particularly lethal. They can level all extant structures with a potential to serve as social expressions of love. They can prevent altogether any new initiatives toward the establishment of a place of refuge. Dispelling disgraceful myths is integral to the work of grace.

22.
Claiming *THE* Model

Whatever grace is, Jesus was full of it. All New Testament writers understand Jesus as the embodiment of grace. None states it more specifically than the author of the Fourth Gospel—"And the Word became flesh . . . full of grace and truth" (John 1:14).

Persons interested in establishing a community of grace find in Jesus the quintessential model for this endeavor. In reality, Jesus is *the* only model for their mission. Jesus is what grace is all about.

Look at Jesus' Actions

Observe the actions of the one "full of grace" and you will receive a good introduction to the character of grace in all of its expressions. Minimally, learning the meaning of grace requires looking at the ministry of Jesus.

Look at Jesus traveling amid dust and sweat to offer redemption to people who did not even want him in their towns. Grace!

Look at Jesus touching people whom every one else labeled unclean and feared to touch. Grace!

Look at Jesus healing individuals who were not thoughtful enough even to say "thank you" for the cure. Grace!

Look at Jesus making a hero of a man who paid the same wage to a poor person who worked for one hour as to poor people who worked all day long. Grace!

Look at Jesus forgiving a woman caught in sin, delivering her from the hands of people about to give her legal justice, and then without qualification sending her home. Grace!

Look at Jesus eating a meal with a man so hated by society that others would not even greet him in public. Grace!

Look at Jesus talking to and accepting nourishment from a woman whom most everybody gossiped about but with whom no one would dare be seen. Grace!

Look at Jesus with his dying breaths praying for the forgiveness of the very people who were humiliating him as they killed him. Grace!

Look at Jesus coming back to love the people from whom he had received hatred and offering redemption to those whose actions had declared, "Get out of our world." Grace!

Look at Jesus intersecting the lives of people who had turned their backs on him and promising to come back again to persons who refused to accept his previous coming and never even invited a second coming. Grace!

God's grace as revealed in Jesus Christ is an overwhelming good. At every turn, beneath every footstep, around every corner, and amid every crisis of people's lives grace abounds. Merit and worth are non-issues. With unrelenting compassion God keeps on offering grace—grace if people will have it, grace every time people need it. God's grace explodes over troubled persons sending particles of mercy to rest on all involved—the scum and the scrubbed-clean of the community; the self righteous, the really righteous, and the unrighteous.

What is the image, the appearance, of a community of grace? Study the personhood and the servanthood of Jesus. Jesus is what grace looks like.

Listen to Jesus' Message

Listen carefully to Jesus' message to hear what grace sounds like. Evident in Jesus' words are both the mood and the content by which grace is best conveyed.

The mood of Jesus' message is that of the indicative rather than the imperative. Right from the start, this was the case. In his inaugural sermon in the synagogue at Nazareth, Jesus announced a time of salvation in which captives will be set free, the blind enabled to see, and the oppressed relieved (Luke 4:18-19). The first time Jesus spoke to the public at large, he also began with an indicative: "The time is fulfilled, and the kingdom of God is at hand" (Mark 1:15).

Imperatives are a part of the message of Jesus (integral to the gospel). But they are always sounded after the divine indicative is declared. A pattern is unmistakable. Jesus mandates, "Repent and believe in the gospel" (Mark 1:15), only after he announces the arrival of God's kingdom. The sequence of Jesus' words is as significant as it is obvious. People do not usher in the kingdom of God by their good works. The kingdom of God is at hand—an act, a gift, of God's grace. Fellowship with God is available to people not because it is a possibility that has been earned or merited by anyone, but because it is an opportunity created by God's grace toward every one.

Disciples of Jesus know well the demands of the gospel. Where there is blessing, there is responsibility. Obedience to the directives of Jesus gives fullness to the life of faith. Such obedience is a product of grace, however, not a prerequisite to grace. Experiencing the gift of God's love, God's people care for the earth as well as for each other, seeking to eliminate abuse and pollution in relation both to individuals and the environment. Recognizing Jesus as the Prince of Peace launches disciples of Jesus into activities aimed at eradicating prejudice, hostility, and violence and establishing reconciliation, practicing forgiveness, and working for peace.

The self-evident order is terribly important. People follow Jesus because they want to, and they are enabled to respond to his grace. Individuals do not obey Jesus because they have to earn his love. In reality, apart from the promise and the power inherent in the indicative from Jesus, no one would ever be able to carry out the imperatives of Jesus.

Unfortunately, contemporary faith communities often invert the indicative-imperative order completely. People are addressed first and foremost with demands—thou shalts and thou shalt nots. As a result of this perverted proclamation, perceptions of faith are distorted. Persons are robbed of the strength as well as the true motivation for faithfulness. Grace seems non-existent.

The indicative—the announcement of God's grace—must come first. Karl Barth once observed that one for whom "this positive task is not absolutely the supreme task, who first of all wants to shout at, bewilder, or laugh at men on account of their folly and malice, had better remain silent altogether."[43] That goes for communities as well as for individuals.

The content of Jesus' message is good news, not bad news. Jesus announces that God loves and accepts all people. Divine love is extended without conditions.

Any downside to the gospel is a human creation. People who prefer for every experience to have its dark dimension can wrangle a shadow even from the bright light of the gospel. Obviously, to reject Jesus' invitation to enjoy fellowship with God is to cut one's self off from meaning, fulfillment, and joy. This is bad news. But such a negative plight in life is experienced only if preferred and accepted by personal choice. Certainly this is not the preference of God or the focus of the message of Jesus. Just the opposite.

God does not have to be satisfied with people's obedience prior to revealing divine love, acceptance, and pleasure for those people. The advent of God's kingdom is not contingent upon the accomplishments of disciples. God loves all people. God accepts all people. God offers all people deliverance from a fretful life filled with a constant striving to earn God's favor. God's grace is assured right up front. God's grace is a given—God's grace to people, for people, and through people.

Any community truly inspired by the ministry of Jesus and gathered around the message of Jesus is brimming with good news. Comfort is extended and assistance is offered to persons beset by bad news. But the bad news is neither imposed nor strengthened by the community. Where grace is present, the news is good.

Jesus is what grace is all about. Nowhere else does grace find so full an expression. In no other person do the social implications of grace receive such careful elaboration. Jesus models grace (he is *the* model of grace) for all people seeking to provide a communal expression of grace.

VII.
Living in a Community of Grace

"In the Kingdom of Mercy, there is always comic surprise as Grace has the last laugh on Justice."

Andrew M. Greeley
Ascent Into Hell

"The just . . . are not stuffy, righteous types with yard-long lists of good works, but simply all the forgiven sinners of the world who live by faith—who just trust Jesus and laugh out loud at the layoff of all the accountants."

Robert Farrar Capon
The Parables of Grace

Grace addresses persons individually. Grace establishes a bond between people that creates community. Personal privacy is respected. Individuality is protected. Isolationism, however, is prohibited. Grace is bent toward society. Grace develops and depends upon community—a community among people built upon the foundation of the relationship (community) that exists between people and God.[44]

Dynamics exist in a community that cannot be duplicated singularly, not even in a one-on-one relationship, as important as that is. The supportive strength derived from a loving fellowship has no substitutes.

Members of a community of grace regularly experience unique ministries of mercy. Whether extending them or receiving them, everyone in such a community is a beneficiary of grace, not only the grace of God, but the grace of people as well.

23.
Identifying Members of the Community

Members of a community of grace almost defy description. No two are identical. Diversity is the rule rather than an exception—diversity in backgrounds, gifts, beliefs, interests, rituals, education, health, talents, economic statuses, social skills, looks, and needs. What unity exists—and a considerable amount of unity is unmistakable—results from grace—everybody's need to receive grace and everybody's interest in sharing grace. Members of a community of grace are benefactors and beneficiaries of mercy.

"Why not identify participants in any grace community with members of a church?" someone asks, assuming the two are synonymous. The question is as beneficial as the equation is harmful. Proceed with care.

Once again, a distinction has to be made between what should be true and what is true. Theologically, every body of believers, every fellowship of God's people, every church is a community of grace. Practically, though, this is not the case. Not every grouping of people claiming the title "church" constitutes a community of grace.

In some instances, congregations retain the label of "church" to denote their identity but reject the essential nature of the church's spirit and ministry in their corporate life. Anyone who confuses such a cultural entity with a biblically-based body whose equivalent is a community of grace runs a risk of being deeply hurt as well as greatly surprised. Turning to this kind of social group for encouragement, assistance, and spiritual sustenance, only to receive reprimands, judgment, and threats of punishment, worsens a troubled person's situation far more than helps it.

A true church rightly claims a special relationship with grace. Indeed, a real church serves as a dispenser of grace. But in some fellowships, something has gone wrong—badly wrong. Reflecting on his spiritual pilgrimage, one seeker of grace wrote in his diary, "The strongest argument *against* Christianity is . . . Christians—when they are somber and joyless, when they are self-righteous and smug in complacent consecration, when they are narrow and repressive."[45] Unfortunately, this man's experience was not unique. Historians identify numerous persons of an international stature as people who, by the scholars' estimates, would have become Christians had it not been for the Christians they met.

Always masterful in his use of analytical skills, Robert Capon writes of how persons who set out to be the church became something else instead:

> We faked her natural multiplicity into a monolithic unity. We pretended that an institution composed entirely of sinners could somehow, as an institution, be pure. We talked ourselves into believing that a crowd of people who by necessity would hardly ever agree even about easy things would infallibly get all the hard things right. We made believe that the Holy Spirit would use a totally political entity without ever letting politics into the act. We turned an absurd, gospel-proclaiming gaggle of geese into an efficient question-answering machine. And we fobbed off on ourselves—we who, like the rest of the race, can barely organize our way out of a wet paperbag—the solemn proposition that, because we were the church, we had access to some divine managerial competence that the world could never have.[46]

In such a situation, regardless of the ecclesiastical terminology used to describe it, grace goes begging. Grace is as scarce in that kind of body as it is in the rest of the world (sometimes more scarce). But, more must be said.

Grace is bigger than any church—whether a body with a pseudonym or the real thing. A community of grace can exist apart from a building characterized by an ethereal architectural design and a program developed and directed by seminary graduates. A fellowship of mercy is not guaranteed by a sign that announces a congregation's denominational affiliation and intention to function as a church. Who are the members of such a fellowship?

Participants in a community of grace are best identified by the ministries of grace they perform.

Friends and Family (Foiled)

Prior to the abrupt ending of his all-too-brief life, Grady Nutt turned a phrase in a prayer that captures a fundamental truth. While expressing gratitude before a meal, Grady thanked God "for family who are friends and for friends who are family." Persons bearing both identities inhabit every community of grace.

Scholars responsible for "Today's English Version" of the Bible chose the term "friend" and the concept of "friendship" to convey the quality of the divine-human relationship made possible by redemption. Translators for this popular version of the scriptures, rendered "reconciliation"—the term most commonly used to denote Jesus' graceful action—as making friends: "God . . . through Christ changed us from enemies into his friends" (2 Cor 5:18, TEV). Likewise, the substance of the message of salvation to be shared with all people is defined as "God making all mankind his friends through Christ" (2 Cor 5:19, TEV). This translation of the Bible enhances both the meaning of redemption and the significance of friendship for its readers. Where grace exists, so does friendship—friendship between individuals and God, friendship among all of God's people.

The term "friend" denotes intimacy. Staples among friends, according to Immanuel Kant, are freedom and loyalty. Friends live for each other, committed to each other unconditionally.

Loyalty among friends is a given. Friendship does not depend upon circumstances (of difficulty or ease), the advantages and disadvantages of the relationship, popularity, or promise. Mistakes, failures, and sins do not threaten the stability of friendships. Just the opposite really. Times of trouble tend to bring friends closer together rather than push them apart. Friends stand by each other come what may.

Friends put away all pretense. Among friends, no one has to be on guard about anything. True friendships continue whether or not right words are being spoken, proper decisions are being made, or appropriate behavior demonstrated. In a fellowship of friends, every person feels free to be whoever she is, to show how she really feels, and to speak what is on her mind with no fear of any rejection of her as a person. To be among friends is to sense the security to let down (or to break down) completely—venting anger, confessing sins, shouting frustrations, mumbling profanities, pacing restlessly, sitting quietly, sobbing uncontrollably. To relate to friends is to climb to new heights emotionally—laughing hysterically, dancing uninhibitedly, excitedly discussing an accomplishment, shouting joyously, running about wildly.

"That sounds very much like the fellowship of a family," someone observes. Right. Precisely. That is the point. Even in biblical terminology, the friends of God make up the family of God——brothers and sisters in faith. Participants in a community of grace are members of a family in which affection and respect join loyalty and freedom.

Uniformity is not a requirement for membership in a family. Identical twins or quadruplets are still unusual from the standpoint of statistics. Radical diversity—emotionally and behavioral as well as physically—is common in a family. No one has to be just like anyone else. Each person is accepted, loved, and supported for who he is.

Failures, mistakes, and moral mishaps do not destroy a family. Actually, such experiences are expected. Healthy families harbor no illusions about the perfection of any person within them or the ease with which good relationships are maintained.

Family members and friends alike recognize relationships that are more important than self will, as valuable as life itself. Each person involved willingly gives up something—small or great—for the betterment of another. The gift may be a piece of clothing or a sum of money or a much more difficult expression of love, such as understanding or forgiveness.

Idyllic images are inappropriate in a vision of a community of grace. All friends who are family are shot through with flaws. A young woman can serve as a close friend with an older gentleman who has been betrayed because one time in a relationship she was a traitor. The tears of a distraught and defamed businessman are encouraged and then dried by a man of the same age who not long before this moment had his bout with frantic sobs of insecurity. No perfection exists here. All the folks in this fellowship have seen their lives foiled in one way or another. Ironically though, the shared weaknesses give the community strength.

Priests and Prophets (Impure)

Linguistically a close relationship exists between the English words "person," "parson," and "priest."[47] Within a community of grace, the roles of these individuals reflect a similar kinship. This situation is of profound significance theologically.

In the New Testament, the term "priest" denotes the spiritual identity of every believer, not an ecclesiastically-selected official. A person does not become a priest by the rites of a religious organization. An individual *is* a priest by virtue of her relationship with God. All of God's people are priests. Persons are to function as priests to each other.[48]

Once again, stereotypical images best be dismissed. Priests adorned in long, flowing ecclesiastical robes highlighted with sparkling pieces of jewelry created out of Christian symbols, voicing ancient liturgies, and mysteriously performing various rituals do not tell the whole story about priesthood. Within a community of grace, an older gentleman wearing an open-neck shirt and tennis shorts takes on the identity of a priest as he listens to an anxiety-riddled colleague pour out confessions of his sins and then speaks words of assurance and pardon. A woman in a business suit performs the priestly functions of intercessory prayer, guidance counseling, and a physical touch of supportive compassion for a man whose haggard appearance is indicative of his beleaguered soul.

A community of grace cannot exist apart from people serving as priests to each other. To function as a priest is not to assume a position of moral superiority in order to help an inferior member of the community. The priest who helps another individual in one area of life needs assistance for herself in a different area. A person who is not hurting at one moment takes care of another who is. Everybody's time will come. A mutuality of priestly ministries maintains the community.

Purity is not a factor. In reality, it never is—not even among those persons whose claim to priesthood rests on an official sacrament or clergy ordination within a church. Priests—all priests—are people— people with the same hang-ups, temptations, problems, and potential as all other people. That is why every priest needs a priest. A priest is just as much an impure human being as the next person. Ironically, in the final analysis, maybe that is the most essential credential for the priesthood—an honest recognition of the imperfect humanity of every person coupled with the conviction that such an individual can serve God as an instrument of grace.

A close relationship exists between priests and prophets. These are not, as once thought, rigid offices positioned at opposite ends of a ministerial dichotomy. In reality, one person can bear both identities within a community.

Often people are put-off by thoughts of prophets—a disheveled, long-haired itinerant who lashes out at establishments and always speaks as if on the verge of an angry rage; a bellowing, dancing, tragic-comic character like Saul; a fearless, though curious, herald of repentance such as John the Baptizer. Individuals understandably decide that they neither need nor want to be prophets shaped in such molds. But, prophets are no more all alike than priests are all the same.

Prophets are truth-tellers. How they look, where they come from, what they have on, the nature of their diet, and the tone of their voices are virtually irrelevant considerations. Most essential is their ministry of truth.

Within a community of grace a prophet is also a friend. And a priest who not only can warn listeners of the destructive consequences of their sins but speak compassionately about the availability of forgiveness. Talking to a man in the midst of a mid-life crisis, a college student serves as a prophet warning his partner in conversation about the devastating emptiness that results from ceaseless sexual promiscuity. A woman sensitively as well as prophetically speaks to a mother sharing wisdom on how to improve her relationship with a disturbed child.

Prophets deal in hope about the good that can be every bit as much as in denunciations aimed at the evil that is. Prophetic negatives are intended to serve the cause of greater positives. Prophets say "no" to one way of life so that "yes" can be said to a better way. Prohibitions in one direction are complimented by affirmations pointed in another direction.

Many of the prophets described in the scriptures model character traits worthy of emulation. Standing in sharp contrast to caricatures that depict a prophet as a "spiritual strong man" or a "cultic bouncer," history pictures Jeremiah identifying with and weeping over the plight of his peers. Imagine how Hosea must have been dying inside, humiliated to the core of his being, as he picked his way through the dirt of the slave market in order to reclaim his wife who had betrayed him and embarrassed him. What love. What grace! Humbly weathering crisis after crisis, Isaiah retained a sensitivity to and an ability, in any context, to plead for the exercise of compassion and reason. Numerous nameless prophets in New Testament communities of faith voiced encouragement and offered consolation as well as called people to repentance. Such are the characteristics of people who nurture each other individually and corporately, who constitute a community of grace.

Any society or fellowship without prophets and priests faces serious trouble. Both priests and prophets are present in a community of grace.

Preachers and Pastors (Imperfect)

Preachers herald good news. Pastors practice care. Pulpits and offices are of little importance in the delivery of their services. The ministry of each is essential in a community of grace.

Amid an avalanche of difficulties, people tend to forget that there is any good news anywhere and especially that there is any good news for them personally. Spokespeople, preachers, perform an important task by pointing to possibilities beyond those defined by human capabilities. They open vistas through which never-before-seen truths can be discovered. Such folks offer reminders of the grace that rushes toward sins, failures, and hurts like blood rushes to a cut in the skin.

Messengers of the good news have to repeat the message faithfully. Some folks fail to hear it. Others listen to the sounds of the words spoken but pay no attention to their meaning. Still other people hear the message with understanding but stop short of believing it. The truth seems too good to be believable ("We are not gullible suckers who will fall for every high-sounding idea that comes along. We learned the hard way, buying into too many spiels already.") Besides, the air waves are filled with multiple messages, several of which directly contradict the gospel of grace.

Capon superbly captures the sense of the most essential sermon to be delivered:

> Christianity starts by telling you that you have no place left to go because you're already home free; and no favor to earn because God sees you in his beloved Son and thinks you're the greatest thing since sliced bread. All you have to do is explore the crazy Mystery of your acceptance.[49]

Who would not delight in serving as the bearer of such news?

Though Frederick Buechner was speaking to persons for whom preaching is a professional discipline, his words on that occasion appropriately address all persons who declare the good news as a part of their responsibilities within a community of grace. Buechner advised: "Preach the overwhelming of tragedy by comedy, of darkness by light, of the ordinary by the extraordinary, as the tale that is too good not to be true."[50] If at any moment a person wonders what can be said to an individual engulfed in troubles, she can, in her own manner, say at least that much.

When properly done, the gospel is shared in love—love for its truth about grace and love for the people in need of its staggering news. Thus, preaching and pastoring go together—proclamation and presence, statements and sensitivity, ideas and identification, comments and comfort, messages and ministries. Neither the traditional rite of ordination nor any other form of ecclesiastical endorsement is a prerequisite to taking up this function. The ability to recognize a person's need and the tendency to give whatever can be gathered to help meet that need are qualifications enough for a person to serve as a pastor.

Finding the right word and the best deed for a particular situation may not always happen. All who serve as pastors and preachers are human beings with weaknesses. Occasionally, an individual finds himself incapable of saying what needs to be said to other people. At times, a pastor can be hurting so badly herself that she is unable to help someone else. This is why the whole community of grace is made up of pastors and preachers.

When one fails or finds herself worse off than the person to be helped, others step in and serve, addressing the person in need and offering grace to the one who is usually a grace-giver. It must be this way. All pastors need pastoring. Every preacher of the gospel needs to hear the preaching of the gospel. Thereby grace is exalted, individuals are healed, and community is nurtured.

At one point in the Old Testament narratives about Moses, the ancient patriarch declares wistfully, "Would that all the Lord's people were prophets, that the Lord would put his spirit upon them" (Num 11:29). Exactly, Moses, but more. Would that all of God's people were family, friends, priests, prophets, pastors, and preachers. That is the makeup, those are the members, of a community of grace.

24.
Adopting a Practical Agenda

An old cliché satirically acknowledges "people who are so heavenly minded as to be of no earthly good." The caricature is certainly not without warrant. It is not applicable, however, to members of a community of grace.

As a theological term, grace prompts a considerable amount of ideological talk. But members of a true fellowship of grace do much more than talk about grace. They practice grace (many times without talking about it at all). Specific acts of practical help comprise the agenda for a grace community.

Grace can be perceived in a person's attitude. Grace can be detected in an individual's manner of speech. Grace can be identified by the spirit that pervades a group. But, no substitutes exist for the communication of grace in redemptive words and deeds. A community of grace cannot risk a misperception or an oversight of its grace among persons in need of refuge. Thus, a spiritual commitment to grace leads to the adoption of an agenda of extremely-practical actions oriented to hurting persons.

A word of warning is in order. Do not confuse a community of grace with a psychiatric clinic, a detoxification center, a mental health institute, or a conventional hospital staffed with medically-trained personnel. To be sure, grace may be present and experienced in all such settings. Distinctions should be made, however, between treatments administered by professional agencies and resources for help available in more informal fellowships.

Not even the very best efforts of persons who constitute a community of grace can take the place of the diagnoses, prescriptions, and therapeutic procedures offered by highly-trained professionals in a clinical context. Not even saturating individuals with grace can bring them healing if their fundamental needs are chemically, biologically, mentally, or emotionally related. As important as its ministry is, a community of grace must realistically face the limits of its contributions to a person's life. Sometimes a fellowship of mercy has to settle for existing as a stand-by community, a caring context available for people to move into and out of while receiving technically-specialized treatment elsewhere.

Here are suggestions regarding the most important items on a practical agenda for a grace-based, God-centered, person-oriented community.

Offer Acceptance

A community of grace exists for everyone willing to live with grace as well as by grace and for all persons in need of grace. Members maintain an open fellowship. Exclusiveness is not allowed. Acceptance is offered to everybody without prerequisites, qualifications, or conditions of any kind.

One exception does exist. Unwelcome in a community of grace are individuals who, because of their rejection of grace, are as uncomfortable in such an environment as they are disapproving of its existence. Neither wanted nor needed in this fellowship are folks who feel compelled to judge, reprimand, shame, correct, or harass in other ways people who have not lived up to (or down to) their expectations. Plenty of other places are available for persons who prefer an existence in which acceptance is dependent upon strict compliance with performance criteria, behavior codes, and other innumerable regulations.

In spirit and content, the openness of a grace-oriented fellowship emulates the blanket invitation to refuge offered by Jesus, the Incarnation of grace. With no reservations, Jesus declared, "Come to me, all who labor and are heavy laden ("who are tired from carrying heavy loads" TEV), and I will give you rest" (Matt 11:28).

Alleviate Fear

Frequently, fear fills the lives of persons in need of a refuge. Watch them repetitively looking back over their shoulders and invariably flinching at even the slightest unexpected sound. Such external actions indicate the nerve-racked state of these people internally.

Probably among the fearful, the very idea of a community of grace seems like an incredible discontinuity given their various experiences of hurt. Trust is virtually non-existent. Relaxation is resisted because letting down one's guard raises the possibility of a vulnerability that is sure to be violated. The worst is expected. Fear itself becomes a source of security for persons concerned about self-protection.

Only with the passing of time in a community of grace can the non-threatening atmosphere of this fellowship be fully realized and trusted. Individuals in search of refuge, however, can be helped immensely by hearing certain statements from community members up front, on the occasion of their first contact. For example: "Welcome. Please know that it doesn't matter why you are here. Our only concern right now is to help you if that is possible." "Anytime you wish to talk, we will be pleased to listen, but none of us will attempt to force you into conversation." "We know what it is to hurt for so long that you begin to live on edge always anticipating more hurt. No one here intends to hurt you. You have no need to worry about any unwelcome surprises—another shoe to drop or a knock-out punch to be thrown." Emotionally massaged by these assurances, slowly, within the refuge-seeker, taut nerves relax a bit, knots in the stomach shrink in size, stress pains in the chest become less frequent, and fear gives way to faith or at least opens the door to that possibility.

Predictably, in most fellowships of mercy, one basic fear haunts members of the community—a fear of abuse. "Someone is going to take advantage of us." "As sure as we continue to exercise grace, people are going to take us for a ride." Usually, this fear is bred by calculating minds interested in the receipt of good dividends for costly investments. "It's bad enough not getting anything in return for our services, let's be sure we don't get used."

A fear of abuse has a basis in facts. Goodness does get abused. People take advantage of fellowships of mercy. Worry about this development, however, is inconsistent with the very nature of grace. Grace cannot be withheld from anyone simply because someone might take unfair advantage of it. Count on abuses of grace from time to time. God calls people to exercise grace faithfully, not to attempt determinations of how people will respond to it.

Listen with Compassion

Listening can be much more important than speaking in the presence of people who are hurting. Often, troubled individuals are worn out from having to repeat explanations of what happened to them, rationalizations about their situations, and statements of their plans. A long expanse of silence may be among the best of a community's immediate gifts to a person in need.

Times for talking will come. Eventually, one who has sought refuge will sense a desire to talk. No one pattern of what comes next is predictable, though. Once speech begins, a lot of different developments can occur.

Anger and resentment may come gushing out in hateful words, gutter expressions, gross generalizations, and curses. Listen. This is no time for a prudish lecture on clean speech.

Depression can cause confessions to be spoken no louder than a near-inaudible whisper. Listen. Don't endanger a continuation of the moment by saying "Speak up louder, I can't hear you."

Obviously untrue accusations and harsh denunciations may be hurled about without restraint or discrimination. Listen. Refrain from immediately challenging the accuracy of a person's charges and from defending the innocence of the people attacked. Occasions for clarification will come later.

Once a troubled individual has spoken, no one needs to feel any compulsion to make a verbal response. If those who have listened do not know what to say, they should not say anything. By all means, no one should attempt to explain whatever wrongdoing is involved or simplistically declare that everything is going to be alright. God needs no defense. Great care should be taken before anyone even says, "I understand" or "I know how you must feel."

A capacity to listen sensitively communicates more grace than ever can be captured in oral comments.

Express Affirmation

Battered bodies are easy to recognize. Tortured spirits may be difficult to discern. A shattered trust, an abused ego, a defeated spirit, or a broken heart, however, can cause just as much pain as a blackened eye, a bruised arm, or a fractured bone. Among most people in need of grace, self-worth is nil, self-confidence is shot, and self-help is difficult if not impossible.

Affirming words and actions affect damaged emotions as a soothing salve on an aching joint, a cool towel on a fevered forehead, or an antibiotic attacking infection. A caring look may suffice in one situation. Or, a touch on the back. Providing a note to be read at a person's own initiative can be beneficial. Many times, a gentle hug is worth more than a cabinet full of medicines.

If not from the beginning of a relationship, at some point in its development, affirming words will be in order: "Making a mistake (or committing a sin) does not destroy your worth as a person." "You are as valuable in God's sight right now as at any other time." "Deprecating estimates voiced by your enemies cannot be allowed to determine your concept of who you are." "You may be better able to live more meaningfully after you recover from this crisis than you eve could have before it occurred." "Please do not lose sight of what you can do."

Why some people think that attacking and tearing down a person is morally beneficial makes no sense. Though certain acts by an individual cannot be, and should not be, affirmed, that individual can be affirmed. Improvement in any one is much more the product of affirmation than of condemnation.

One Sunday morning I was elated to see a friend show up for a Bible Study class. I knew he was in desperate need of a supportive fellowship strengthened by faith. My spirit quickly plummeted, however. The wife of the class's teacher approached my friend and loudly said, "Well, I hope the ceiling of the church doesn't fall in because you're here." Naturally, my friend was embarrassed and repulsed. As far as I know, he did not ever return. A word affirming his presence could have made a huge difference for good in this man's life.

Jesus repeatedly revealed the affirming nature of grace. He said to a lame man, "Get up and walk" (not "Now you may not be able to do this, but I want you to try to take a step."). Jesus told an adulteress, "Go and sin no more" (not "How could you have done such a thing? You are evil. But, try not to let it happen again."). Jesus commended a father who said to a son who had left home in a huff: "I'm so glad you are back. I have missed you. We need you here" (not "Listen, you better get this immorality corrected and set up a plan by which you can repay the money you have wasted if you want to earn a right to be a part of this family again.").

A person has not truly experienced grace until she knows that she has value and is valued (not the promise or the possibility, but the reality of value).

Practice Patience

Few wounds heal quickly. Especially is this the case for troubled minds, guilt-ridden consciences, disturbed emotions, and splintered spirits. Though grace always hurries to a person in need, grace is never in a rush to get away and get on with something else.

The kinds of problems that precipitate major crises in people's lives usually have been present for a long time (often a life time). No quick fix is possible. Assurances of welcome and acceptance, as well as words of affirmation and encouragement, may have to be repeated again and again.

Unfortunately, grace is so rare and communities of grace are so scarce in our society that learning to live in grace, by grace, and with grace is somewhat akin to a space traveler trying to adjust to a totally new atmosphere. Patience is important.

God's patience is a major attribute of divine mercy!

Expand Vision

Deeply troubled people typically become nearsighted—unable to see clearly, if at all, anything existing beyond the boundaries of their problem. Mumbled confessions reveal the narrow scope of their limited vision. "I will never trust another man." "Love just sets you up for betrayal." "People are never going to let me forget my sin." "I have failed again; I am doomed to failure." "I never will be able to get another job." "I am finished in this community." "Joy is impossible." "I see no way out of this awful grief."

An expansion of a nearsighted person's vision is a great contribution to the relief of hurt and depression—lifting sights above a consuming anger or beyond a debilitating grief. To make problem-weary people aware of unexpected opportunities for relief and to introduce them to the growth experiences of other persons once in their situation are like lifting heavy window shades and allowing invigorating sunlight to pour into a dingy, dark, and depressing room. Enabling a person to see a way through intimidating difficulties is akin to knocking down the walls of a prison and introducing freedom to the captives.

Simply discovering that they are not alone in their dilemmas can be of inestimable worth for hurting people. Eyes brighten as they look into the faces of supportive people who, having made their ways through dark valleys and found light both without and within, are now ready to assist others (them) entrapped in shadows.

A truly expanded vision nurtures a realization of the presence of God. Within a community of grace, fatigued folks find evidence that the world is inhabited by a God ready to meet individuals amid their problems and to call out compassionate people to be of help as well. Those who pay careful attention may well hear from one who finds refuge among them a contemporary counterpart to the declaration of an ancient shepherd— "Thou art with me; thy rod and thy staff, they comfort me" (Ps 23:4).

Another name for expanding people's vision is giving people hope. A community of grace is a community of hope. Beneficiaries of such a fellowship experience a strengthening of their spirits along with an enhancement of their sight.

Share Burdens

Full participation in a community of grace involves a willingness to receive what is readily given. Individuals eager to demonstrate grace to others in need are challenged to open themselves to the grace available from those served.

Sharing burdens is a two-way street. Sometimes, it is easier to assist someone else than to submit to being assisted. Responding to vulnerability is far less difficult than displaying vulnerability. Yet, in many instances, a major gift of grace is the creation of an opportunity for the one being served to serve.

Superiority is a nonsequitor in considerations of a community of grace. Perfection and self-sufficiency are nonexistent. At one time or another, every member of the fellowship has to wrestle with a heaviness that is best handled by being shared. Little wonder that the wise apostle from Tarsus commended commitment to a fellowship marked by complete reciprocity—"Bear one another's burdens" (Gal 6:2).

Encourage Ministry

Critically ill people require constant care. As healing takes place in their lives, however, less and less uninterrupted attention to them is needed. A full recovery of good health involves the discovery of a desire for extending care to others as well as receiving care from others. If, for some reason, a person gets locked into a disposition in which what is received is all that matters, a substantial amount of illness remains within her.

It is not uncommon for troubled people to become extremely self-centered—preoccupied with the pain inflicted upon them and the gnawing hurt within them and concerned that everybody else understand the uniqueness of their situation. Usually unaware of their condition, such people talk about themselves incessantly. They show virtually no awareness of, much less concern for, the presence of persons, especially burdened persons, around them.

People who have been besieged by difficulties can be made to understand that they are especially equipped to aid others under a similar siege. Facilitating such a recognition and its subsequent services is extremely important. This is the manner in which individuals are significantly benefitted and a community of grace is enabled to function—grace receivers become grace givers. (No assumption is made that anyone will ever move beyond periods of personal need in which the reception of care from others is important. At stake is only a suggestion regarding the importance and effectiveness of "wounded healers.")

When persons who have received help begin seeking to be helpful, they make important strides toward strength and good health in their lives and toward the enhancement of actions of grace within the community of which they are a part.

Exhibit Laughter

A call for sighs and tears is needless. They will come. As people unravel their various stories and expose the raw edges of their emotions, weeping will take place. This is healthy. But tears and smiles, sobs and laughs, come from the same place within a person. One should not receive attention to the exclusion of the other. Within a community where weeping is predictable, laughing—surprising, unstoppable, uproarious, body-shaking laughter—is essential.

Pervaded with multiple disturbing difficulties in need of grace, life gets unbearably heavy, unduly overloaded with solemnity and severity. In such a situation, people begin to view every word and act with a sense of ultimacy. This is not healthy.

In a community, grace is most apparent when comedy is intermingled with tragedy, when good humor accompanies shared love. Sometimes joking about a problem can be as important as analyzing it. Even satire is appropriate as people learn to laugh at their own mistakes as well as to move beyond them. The presence of hurt does not have to mean a complete absence of laughter. In fact, an inducement to laughing is among the holiest of gifts in a therapy governed by grace.

Practice Flexibility and Spontaneity

Grace produces no one program of care that can be applied to all troubled people. Just the opposite, really. Grace relates to every individual individually. What is most helpful to one person may be of no benefit at all to another person. Grace, then, disdains rigidity— attitudinally, programmatically, and methodologically.

My suggested agenda for a grace community is no exception to the above observation. At best, these recommendations provide grace-motivated people a place to begin in their corporate actions of mercy. If at any point, any part of this agenda fails to facilitate help, it should be discarded quickly and a new plan of care developed. The goal of a grace community is not fidelity to any one plan of action but compassionate responses to all people in need.

Jesus refused confinement to a static pattern of words and acts in ministry. His approaches to help and healing varied as did the sick and troubled people he encountered.

Sometimes a whole new order of services (unplanned) may have to be constructed on the spot for grace to be experienced. No problem. The liberty to act creatively is inherent in the grace that motivates ministry. A commitment to flexibility and spontaneity makes the activity of grace completely unpredictable. The only certainty within a community of mercy is a God-breathed compassion that will not rest until grace has been extended to those who need it most.

VIII.
A Giving Up Place

"God . . . enjoys surprises, twists and turns, kinks and ironies, and happy endings. Ultimately anyway."

Andrew M. Greeley
All About Women

"The eternal afternoon's awkwardness gives way to grace, and the evening of everlasting laughter begins."

Robert Farrar Capon
The Youngest Day

Sitting in a small, uncomfortably warm room in Shanghai, China, one morning, I listened to a young pastor speak about the various ministries of his vibrant congregation. Members of this fellowship were all-too-well acquainted with hurt, having survived Chairman Mao's extended persecution of religious communities. Now permitted to function as a church once again, these people who had been through a "long dark night" were reaching out to individuals in need of them. Someone in our small group of visitors asked, "What kind of church is this?" "Christian," the minister responded. Momentarily another person spoke up, "What is the name of this church?" "Grace," the pastor said.

"Grace Church!" The thought exploded in my head and shook my spirit. "What an absolutely wonderful idea." I could not let go of the concept. "Not Grace Presbyterian Church or Grace Catholic Church. No other qualifiers. Just Grace Church." Then came the stinging question that still lingers: "Is it possible?"

I knew then as I know now that grace and church should be, but are not, synonymous terms. The reality is that in contemporary experience, one can exist without the other. However, I have not been able to turn loose of that idea of a body of believers known only by the title of "Grace." Continued meditation on a community of grace births the conclusion of this book.

25.
No Cheap Grace

Ever since the publication of Dietrich Bonhöffer's scathing critique of "easy Christianity" in *The Cost of Discipleship,* comments about grace have been profitably evaluated by this Christian martyr's expose of "cheap grace." More than merely helpful, Bonhöffer's insights are crucial to people seeking to establish a community of grace.

Graceless voids in ecclesiastical and social fellowships do not need to be filled with a counterfeit commodity. Nothing would be gained by that development. Grace is a gift and thus inherently free. But, grace is costly, invariably very costly. Building a strong community of grace requires sparing no expense.

Bonhöffer equated "cheap grace" with grace understood only as a doctrine, a principle, or a system. "Cheap grace" requires from its proponents only intellectual affirmation and a very general application of its meaning to life. Conversely, "costly grace" demands a total discipleship dedicated to Christ. "Cheap grace" allows for personal behavior to remain unchanged by an encounter with it. Both sins and sinners are justified when grace is cheap. Advocates of "cheap grace" look and live like everybody else. In contrast, "costly grace" justifies sinners but condemns sins. Adherents to "costly grace" embrace a life style distinctive as that of a Christian disciple.[51]

The grace required to build a community of refuge is in no sense cheap. Not a *carte blanche* for sin, as charged by people paranoid about compassion, grace goes to every extreme to defeat sin. Far from taking morality lightly, grace deals with morality so seriously that it seeks a righteousness impossible by obedience to legal precepts alone. Grace posits that a provision of forgiveness, restoration, and continued encouragement for those who have sinned is important enough to justify real sacrifices on the part of the innocent. (This can only mean those who are innocent in the situation under consideration. Everybody has a time of guilt.)

Grace in action is never cheap. At a minimum, grace creates nerve-racking vulnerability as it seeks to make love a reality. Often grace is misunderstood and sometimes even attacked when help is extended to victimizers as well as to victims. Characteristically, grace involves bearing the pain and living through the hell caused by someone else's deeds. Grace bears the brunt of angry criticisms agitated by self-appointed judges of morality who fear that a sinner may be spared the worst possible punishment. Grace advocates reconciliation when extending forgiveness to a wrongdoer is so painful as to be almost unbearable. Grace agrees to live in and with scandal if scandal is a consequence of being graceful. Grace is not cheap. A community of grace can never be built at bargain prices.

A recent conversation helped me better understand Bonhöffer's distinction between "cheap grace" and "costly grace." The dialogue would have been humorous had not the issue involved been so serious.

Two relatives were talking about a family member presently in a tough situation. All three are faithful church members. As one aunt described the problematic plight of their nephew, the other aunt responded with a barrage of pietistical clichés: "He just needs to trust God. Tell him we will pray with him about his difficulty. God will work everything out if the boy just has enough faith." She went on and on. Noting her sister's impatience, the speaker felt the need to explain that she and her husband had become "fundamentalist Christians" (her term). The aunt who initiated the talk about the nephew said, "Well, he is a Christian, but he is not a fundamentalist." At that, the more verbal aunt said, "Oh well, then, we will not be able to help him."

Even grace that is lauded by the most orthodox (from the perspective of a "fundamentalist") believer betrays itself as "cheap grace" if it sets up exceptions, develops restrictions, and defines extenuating circumstances that justify it being withheld from a person in need. Grace is for fundamentalists and liberals, skeptics and conservatives, narrow-minded fanatics and open-minded seekers, optimists and pessimists—everybody. Differences in beliefs and points of view may make an exercise of grace more difficult. But if it were easy, it would not be grace.

Real grace always costs plenty. The time is never right for it. Usually prevailing political sentiments oppose it. Controversy surrounds it. Criticisms accompany it. Seemingly insurmountable problems constitute the natural environment in which grace functions.

In any situation, the depth of the difficulties confronting grace reveals why grace is needed. Grace is not an issue where all is well. Problematic, tough applications of grace reveal a major dimension of what makes grace. That which makes grace necessary makes grace costly.

Whenever the cost of grace is in question, direct the attention of all interrogators to the crucifixion of Jesus. The excruciating suffering of an absolutely innocent man and death willfully accepted by one who came to give life—that is the price of grace (as well as the epitome of the spirit and substance of grace). Never imagine that the formation of a community of grace—a fellowship of acceptance and forgiveness, restoration and new hope, love and mercy—is either easy or cheap. But, keep in mind that in the provision of such a refuge is indescribable joy.

26.
Grace and Guts

Living by grace takes guts. No substitutes suffice. Working with others to build a community of grace, like functioning as a medium of grace individually, requires an emotional commitment to grace. This is not the same as a rational understanding of grace. Not by a long shot. Lofty thoughts about the implementation of grace are distinctly different from (and no guarantees of) gutsy actions that make grace a reality.

Several conversations in recent months have shaken my confidence in reason. They also have raised serious questions in my mind about the relation of theology to life.

In the private dining room of an elitist social club in a major southern city, I met the president of an insurance company for lunch. He wanted to talk about a problem related to his church. Specifically, he desired counsel on how to steer a personnel committee to take redemptive action on behalf of a troubled minister.

After nearly two hours of conversation and what seemed to be an excellent "meeting of the minds," we went our separate ways. Three days later, the man phoned me to report on his committee's decision. After a lengthy discussion, members of the personnel committee concluded that the minister in question was "too controversial" for their church. I wondered to myself how a church can ever conform to the gospel without being controversial.

The committee's decision disappointed me. When the caller reported the comments of various committee members, however, I was grieved (and angered). One lady said, "There is no doubt in my mind about what is the Christian thing to do." Another person observed: "I know we ought to act on behalf of this man's welfare. But, we just don't need any debate in the church right now." A man joined in support, "This is not the time for us to risk any criticism within the church."

Over an evening meal in a city in the northeast, a similar conversation took place. In this instance, my role was that of a friendly listener, not a professional consultant. A husband and wife related to me the process by which their congregation had fired their pastor a few weeks earlier. Speaking of their church as a fellowship committed to grace and using the language of grace, these church officers told me a tale of disgrace.

At an informal gathering near my home, I listened to a lay leader of a community church talk to a group of friends about his congregation's difficult dilemma regarding a ministry to victims of AIDS. In reaction to a proposal about such a ministry, several voices protested the thought of their church taking any initiative to help "those kinds of people." A few folks forthrightly declared their opposition to people with AIDS even visiting in their worship services. As a footnote, they indicated that if their wishes were not respected, they might leave the church.

After the pastor of that congregation announced that he would address the subject of AIDS from the pulpit, he was "officially" asked not to do so. Several church members claimed that they had a right not to have to listen to "this mess" in church.

A few people took the interesting approach of opposing an AIDS-related ministry by reasoning that the church needs to serve as a good example in the community. "We can't give recognition to individuals involved in an evil lifestyle." I pondered what those people wanted the church to be a good example of. Certainly not a gospel-shaped community of grace.

Later, when I had a moment alone with this church leader, I inquired about his own views on the matter. Immediately a pained look covered his face. His words were heavy with pathos: "I know what we ought to do. I want our church to reflect the grace of Jesus. But." His voice broke as tears formed in his eyes. When he continued, he said, "That's not who we are as a church. We have too many people who do not relate grace to situations such as this one."

In an effort to help a person with mounting needs, I turned to two longtime friends. Each of these persons has tutored me on the subject of grace. Both have lectured and published on grace. I have benefitted immensely from their insights.

First, I spoke with the CEO of a major organization that advertises itself as a "Christian institution." As I talked about our deeply-troubled mutual friend, I noticed immediate discomfort in the executive. Before I finished detailing for him the nature of our friend's need and the way in which I hoped help could be offered, the CEO interrupted. He told me how much he would like to help. "There's nothing I would like better" were his words. The institutional officer, however, then explained how the timing, environment, and public relations concerns were all wrong right now. As our conversation ended, I acknowledged the difficulties involved in my request and then asked, "How does your theology of grace apply to this situation?" He shrugged his shoulders, smiled, shook his head, and mumbled, "Damned if I know."

A second conversation was similar. In fact, I was still seeking assistance for the same person about whom I had talked with the CEO. This time, my listener was a local leader in a major denomination. He really did not even have time to talk about the matter. As for grace, he did not see that our friend deserved it.

The cumulative effect of all of these conversations was extremely disturbing. Every one of the people with whom I had spoken was an individual who claimed a strong theology of grace. "But, what difference does it make?" That was (is) my question. What is the value of a carefully worked out theology of grace if a person does not have the guts to translate ideas into actions?

I am disenchanted with reason. As far as behavior is concerned, knowledge is overrated.

Education "took" with me. I became enamored with intellectual development and rational processes. For many years, my response to virtually every challenging situation was essentially the same: "Let's think about it."

My assumption was that the key to responsible action is a well-informed intellect finely tuned to sort out all appropriate options, evaluate them, and chart the right direction. I tried to ignore human emotions. When that was not possible, I worked to repress emotions or attempted to set them aside. Dangerous clichés had been internalized as worthwhile convictions: "Let's don't get emotional about anything important." "Be careful not to allow your emotions to get in the way and cloud your decision-making."

I was wrong. Actually, education was not the problem. Formal education was of inestimable worth for me. I just did not have enough of it. I embraced part of the truth and thought I knew all of it. Human beings are rationale creatures. I learned that lesson well and passed every examination question about it. But, seldom, if ever, are people's actions based on reason alone. Emotions are tremendously influential in personal behavior. I missed that point and subsequently failed several real life tests related to it.

In reality, the more significant a decision or an action is in an individual's life, the more prominent will be the role of emotions in determining what develops. Friendships, religious beliefs, love affairs, priorities, marriages, loyalties, and the like are far more profoundly impacted by feelings than by thoughts, by emotions than by intellectual analyses. This truth is not missed by even an academic giant who prized intellectual maturity and rational processes more than most people. Paul Tillich wrote, "Man is fully rational only on the foundation of, and in interdependence with, nonrational factors. . . . Whether called 'instinct' or 'passion' or 'libido' or 'interest' or 'urge' or 'will to power' they cannot be denied."[52]

Throughout this volume, I have tried to make sense. And to cause grace to make sense. My approach to innumerable practical difficulties and ordinary problems has been to present a reasonable explanation as to why grace is the best, most logical response. Undergirding my work with the biblical material is the hope that if people who believe the Bible can understand what the Bible really says about grace, they will move to be more graceful in their lives. A similar idea serves as the foundation for my study of the words and deeds of Jesus. Surely, if Jesus is an individual's Lord, that individual will want to embody the grace that Jesus commends and incarnates. That makes sense. It is reasonable.

I still believe all of that is important. But, it is by no means the whole story. Apart from a gut-level commitment to grace, what a person knows about grace may make only a minimal difference in the way that person lives. Knowing is not doing. And doing depends to an incredible extent on feeling. Necessary, then, is an emotional inclination to live by grace. Grace must be as much a part of a person's instincts as of her thoughts.

Watch a father dash into the flaming inferno of a burning house to see if his young daughter is out and if not to save her. Apply the principle of reason's power here. Did that parent stand in the glow of the blaze and carefully think through his actions? Do you suppose he calculated the risk-potential related to his efforts? Did he do a quick run-through of all the intellectual arguments for and against his various options? No. A negative answers each of these questions. The man's rescue attempt was not logical. His assumptions and motivations may not have been intellectually sound. The father acted out of an immeasurable love. He rushed into danger in reaction to a surge in his gut. He faithfully, even if foolishly, followed the directives of his heart. The man's most fundamental instinct was to attempt a rescue.

This is the instinct formed by grace—rescue. Another word for it is redemption. People of grace move to rescue people in trouble. Often they may not even think about what they are doing. The impulses of grace come as much from the gut as from the head. And by the way, chances are good that acting on the impulse of grace will never seem logical.

As always, history is instructive. Events from recent history powerfully address this matter of the role of reason in exemplary actions.

Remember the showdown in Tianimon Square. Such bravery among advocates for democracy has seldom been seen. But how much sense did it all make? What kind of reasoning motivated those students to take on the whole political power structure in Mainland China? Did it make good sense for a few students to join hands and form a blockade intended to stop onrushing military tanks? What wisdom measures how ideas will fare against guns? None of it was reasonable.

What happened on that expanse of concrete that spreads out in front of Chairman Mao's open coffin was not about the sovereignty of the rational. It was an emotional demonstration undergirded by convictions with guts. Whether or not all the flag waving, singing students in that square could satisfactorily define democracy and elaborate a philosophy of democratic government acceptable to a political science professor, I don't know. But, their commitment to democracy was never in question. And, they exhibited perfectly freedom's reaction to oppression.

Even more recently, when Boris Yeltzin climbed on top of an enemy tank in Moscow and called for massive resistance to the newly formed central government of the Soviet Union, he appeared strong in courage and weak in wisdom. More "good reasons" existed for this man to stay quiet than for him to do or to say anything at all. Then, ordinary citizens used their bodies to block the paths of military tanks. Think about it. Crazy! And, they sought to turn back armed soldiers with only their stubborn presence. How does all of that stand up under rational analysis? In what way did it make sense for those people to risk their lives in the face of weapons-wielding opposition? In the early moments of that dramatic confrontation, hardly anyone gave them the slightest chance of succeeding.

What was in evidence in the shadow of the Kremlin during those tense late summer evenings was a demonstration of how a vision of liberty reacts to threats of tyranny. Maybe principles of democracy filled the minds of some of those resistors. But, they erected human barricades and placed their lives on the line because of what was in their guts. A passion for freedom enflamed actions aimed at creating a new kind of community. As long as history is remembered, those Moscovites' valiant witness to the value of liberty will be celebrated.

Reason alone cannot sustain those kinds of actions. All realizations of both democracy and liberty require much more than an admirable ideology. Courageous deeds are required.

Similarly, reason alone cannot properly motivate grace. Instincts, hunches, and emotions are the crucial components in effecting quick rescues of persons in desperate straits and in adopting longrange plans to build a place of refuge, to provide a community of grace, for all who need mercy.

Strange. Grace makes sense from a theological perspective. Doctrinal thought devoid of a strong emphasis on grace is usually considered grossly deficient. Practically though, grace never seems to make sense. In situations of difficulty, people can always amass more "good reasons" for not acting on grace than for following its directives. What they know as sound doctrine appears irrelevant to what they feel to be the best response to a difficult situation. Their plea is "Let's be reasonable. We must live in the real world." The first line of their litany of justification (rationalization) is usually the same: "I know what grace would have us do." An appropriate ending is selected from several options: "But it is simply too big a risk for us." "But we can't jeopardize people's positive feelings about us." "But that might cost us a bundle of money." "But that is no way to run a business."

Grace-filled actions spring from both good theology and intestinal fortitude. Oddly enough though, if one of these two is weaker than the other, grace usually fares much better as an instinct than as a doctrine. Instincts do the obvious. Doctrines have to be explained.

Acting on grace requires creative innovation. Grace steps into situations that appear unalterably bad and goes to work to bring something positive out of them—for the guilty as well as the innocent. Grace inserts itself into the rhythmic cycle of evil, breaks the predictable repetition of it, and replaces evil with good. Grace turns the other cheek when slapped. Grace goes a second mile when traversing the first mile was done under duress. Grace restores communication between persons who have turned their backs on each other in hostile silence. Grace demands redemption rather than retaliation in response to one who has inflicted hurt. Grace is innovative.

Because the environments in which people most need to receive grace are inevitably problem-plagued and controversial, the practice of grace is never an easy option. Always a house is on fire, a storm is raging, a battle is brewing, a lynch mob is forming, or a bomb has exploded. Reputations, careers, and maybe even lives are threatened. Risks have to be taken and boldness exhibited. Criticisms are probably inevitable. Costs can be high. Reason dictates an alternative—a way around grace. More times than not, grace looks like sheer stupidity. (Keep in mind the foolishness of the cross, the scandal of God seeking to redeem people who act in opposition to redemption.)

Living by grace involves taking chances by acting on questionable hunches rather than forever doing the sure thing. Exercising grace requires getting out on the proverbial limb with a person who never should have been there in the first place, knowing that it could be cut off (maybe even watching saws-armed critics climb the tree eager to sever this troublesome limb from the tree trunk). Demonstrating grace means practicing vulnerability rather than playing it safe. Safer, surer bets are not an option for grace. Take away the risk, controversy, cost, and criticism, and grace too is gone.

Grace is synonymous with gutsy action. Few, if any, applaud it immediately because mercy extends help to people who do not deserve it and offers loving kindness to troubled folks who may not even ask for it. Grace causes a person to shoulder difficulties she has always avoided and to act for the good of others when doing nothing appears to be the better part of wisdom. Grace catapults an individual into problematic situations that could easily and understandably be avoided.

Grace requires a strength fit to face resistance, resilient even amid discouragement, and persistent despite energy-draining criticism. Grace measures situations with criteria birthed in the heart rather than by principles formulated in the head. Sound arguments for calling a halt to acts of mercy or building a community of grace always outweigh reasons to continue. Grace is possible only among persons who don't mind looking to most of the world like fools.

Grace has to take on disgrace unapologetically. Most of the time the speed with which folks can bring grace into a difficulty is hampered by their having to traverse a quagmire of judgmental muck stirred up and spread out by folks who envision themselves as God's only hope for executing moral justice. Sometimes, practitioners of grace must confront out loud the hypocrisy of persons who compound others' problems in the name of righteousness (vindictiveness actually). When punishment-wielding individuals are hiding behind claims of an appreciation for grace, they must be told to put their actions where their mouths are. A moment may come when servants of grace have to tell those people blocking ministries of grace to take their disgrace and go to hell. The words are spoken not as an angry curse or as a slap in the face with a slang expression but as a compassionate, courageous statement of truth. Reasonable, theological truth at that. Hell is created by persons opposed to grace. Hell is where disgrace belongs.

Grace cannot be sustained by reason. Grace takes guts.

How does it happen? Good theology can be taught. Open minds can be instructed in the ways of grace. But how does grace become a part of a person's instincts? How does grace take up residence in human emotions? Whence comes a passion for grace that will not be stifled even by hurt?

A new being is the answer, a quality of life that the apostle Paul calls a "new creation." But this is not an achievement attainable by human effort. Creation is the work of God. A new creation is the work of God in Christ. Living with grace in relation to others is a result of living in (and by) the grace of God. Such life can be experienced only if received as a gift from God.

Life is saturated with grace when life is oriented to God. Grace becomes an integral part of a person's thoughts, intentions, emotions, intuitions, commitments, instincts, and ideas when that person loves God with all of her heart, soul, strength, and mind. God is grace.

Loving God and becoming filled with grace are not laborious tasks. They are like returning home after a long journey when home is where you would rather be than any other place on earth. Opening one's self to God (and thus to grace) is like sprinting across a greening meadow on an early spring day and exulting in the warmth of the sun as it drives away the chill of a too long winter. Allowing grace to saturate your life is akin to standing just off an ocean-side beach on a hot summer afternoon and feeling the cooling but exhilarating sensation of a large rapidly-breaking wave wash across your whole body.

God offers the possibility of a life of grace to everyone through Jesus Christ (our home, the sun of spring time, the incoming wave). However, not all persons want such a life. Some actually refuse it. But, for those who accept, those who really are made new in Christ, living by grace becomes as natural as breathing.

The people of God brought together by Christ are folks who cannot rest until they offer a community of grace as a residence for all in search of mercy. A passion for providing a grace community pervades every aspect of their beings. Minds and hearts. Thoughts and emotions. Intentions and actions.

27.
Refuge and Grace

Alright. So much for elaborations of the need, basis, possibilities, and proposal for a community of grace. An inescapable question is, "Have you ever seen one?" Is the central concern of the preceding pages, the concept of a community of grace, a figment of a vivid imagination, the product of noble aspirations, or does the reality of such a fellowship have any historical documentation?

Naturally, anyone's answers to those inquiries will be shaped by personal experiences. My response to the basic question is affirmative. Yes, communities of grace have existed and do exist. Their number is by no means impressive quantitatively. Eye-catching numerical statistics, however, are not required for significant ministry to take place.

New Testament records reveal the existence of early communities of grace. Most prominent among them was the fellowship constituted by Jesus and the Twelve. Unarguably, not all of the disciples of Jesus modeled grace consistently. At times these men were at each other's throats. The fact that Jesus was the one who brought them together and held them together, however, guaranteed grace in their midst.

Actually, all grace communities form and persist that same way. God's initiative for redemption pervades the lives of people who might otherwise care nothing at all for grace or for each other. Despite the presence of normal human tendencies that disrupt fellowships, the members' relationship with God conditions their relationships with each other and their on-going concern for others. Often in such groups, people are involved who never even would have come together, much less stayed together, had it not been for their need for grace and the call of God. Thus, grace prevails in unlikely places among configurations of people that evoke surprise.

One of the most astounding statements in all of the scriptures is a description of the primitive community of faith in Jerusalem. Reporting on the common life of those early Christians, Luke remarks, almost incidentally, "There was no one in the group who was in need" (Acts 4:34 TEV). Incredible! Perhaps Luke's reference was to material needs alone—food, shelter, clothing. Even that would be remarkable. The sense of the scriptural sentence, however, is that people were taking care of each other completely. If that was the case, this was an exemplary community of grace.

Historians provide glimpses of grace communities that have come and gone through the intervening centuries. The Oxford Groups of a prior day and innumerable units of Alcoholics Anonymous in the present represent the great variety of sacred and secular expressions of fellowships of grace.

At times, an institutional church functions as a community of grace. Many contemporaries cite the Church of the Savior in Washington, D. C., as a prime example of such a fellowship. I agree.

Recently a friend told me about the decision-making process of a deep South congregation seeking a pastor. The final choice was between two men very different in age and experience. The older of the two had been through a difficult divorce and an avalanche of criticism that intensified with his remarriage. The younger of the two was a kind of ministerial "Mary Poppins"—almost too good to be true. The church invited as its pastor the older gentleman with a tainted pilgrimage. Committee members explained that through this action the church could minister to their new pastor as well as request ministry from him. Grace!

Surely, Howard Thurman must have experienced the grace of that type of congregation in his last pastorate. This remarkable thinker-preacher wrote in his autobiography, "There has not been a single day since the beginning of the church that I have not been moved by its spirit. For a breathless moment in time, a little group of diverse people was caught up in a dream as old as life and as new as a hope that just emerges on the horizon of becoming man. "[53]

Frankly, until very recently, this has not been my experience. Most of my encounters with grace in an ecclesiastical setting have come in relation to a church within a church. Small groups formed by persons first brought together by their common interest in the larger group (the institutional church) offer ministries of grace that not only are unavailable in the broader fellowship but often are actually opposed by its "official" structures of leadership. My situation is not unique.

Through the years, I have encountered innumerable individuals involved in a desperate search for a community of grace because of their dysgraceful (or disgraceful) treatment by various bodies of people claiming either to be "church" or "church-related." Reflection on this matter of persons of grace and ecclesiastical institutions underscores the apparently timeless validity of Augustine's ancient assessment: "Many whom God has, the Church does not have; and many whom the Church has, God does not have."[54]

But do I believe communities of grace exist? Yes. Sometimes in a church. Sometimes in a church within a church. Sometimes in a setting with no trappings of the sacred.

My family—extended, generally, but immediate, specifically—has been the primary community of grace in my life. Among these three people I have been accepted when unacceptable, comforted when reprimands would have been more natural, encouraged to laugh when happiness was scarce, loved when unlovable, and cared for when everybody could justifiably have said, "Take care of yourself."

Oh, I know the old cliché, "Blood is thicker than water." But, that is not a valid explanation for what I have experienced. My wife and sons have a gut-level sense of grace, born of their faith I think, and the courage to offer mercy even amid difficulty. Judy, John Paul, and James know how to do experientially what I have tried to describe here literarily. And, I continue to be the much blessed beneficiary of their grace.

My friends form a dedicated, though diasporic, community of grace. Times together personally are far less frequent than long distance telephone calls and occasional pieces of correspondence. What a gift, however, to pick up a telephone receiver and hear a familiar voice say, "I care. Is there anything I can do to help?"

Most of my friends use traditional religious language sparingly, if at all. But they leave no doubt about where and from whom they learned of grace. The depth of their understanding of grace is most obvious in their demonstrable actions, not their theoretical convictions.

In recent months (long after the last page of this manuscript had been typed), I have come to know the unmitigated joy of a church whose vision and mission involve grace. Like many other persons, I have found Northminster Church in Monroe, Louisiana, to be a community of grace.

Refuge is a reality. In a context of grace, insecurities are set aside and anxieties relieved. Nothing is expected of those who enter. Guards come down as defenses dissolve. The edginess sharpened by endless questions about what has happened is blunted by the assurance that no one is going to ask about anything because the content of the past is not a precedent upon which the future is discussed. Paranoia is put away as the realization dawns that "no one here is out to get me or do me in."

Emotions are released without reticence—a rage of anger, a surge of grief, a series of breath-taking sobs accompanied by tears, remorse blurted out with defensiveness, hurt so deep that words cannot communicate it, hope sounded in bursts of great laughter. Relaxation leads to a deep sleep. The soul experiences healing. Energy is reborn. Resolve emerges. Grace is extended to others as lavishly as it has been received.

A refuge may or may not have walls. Grace is not in a place, but in people. Thus, grace instantly, serendipitously, can form a community on the very spot of any difficulty. Where sin, failure, hurt, and other problems abound, grace abounds more.

In *The Diary of a Country Priest,* George Bernanos writes of beneficence in the face of the dominance of its opposites. Toward the end of the novel, Bernanos describes a poverty-stricken *cure* who is dying of cancer. As his death grows imminent, the Cure is told that he will have to die without receiving the sacrament of extreme unction, in his faith the most important bestowal of ultimate meaning on his life and death. No priest can arrive in time to administer the sacrament. The response of the Cure is so surprising as to seem scandalous—"Does it matter?" Then he explains the meaning of his reaction, saying, *"Tout est grace"* ("All is grace"). The beautiful English translation of that phrase is the conclusion of this book: "Grace is everywhere."[55]

Grace is everywhere!

"May the grace of the Lord Jesus be with everyone."
(Rev 22:21, TEV)

Notes

[1]Jonathan Coleman, *Exit The Rainmaker* (New York: Atheneum, 1989).

[2]*Ibid.*, 40.

[3]*Ibid.*, 122.

[4]Residents of a city of refuge were required to remain within the precincts of the city until the death of the high priest. At that time, they were at liberty to relocate as they willed.

[5]Official responses to wrongdoers changed with time within Israel. Earliest were the vendettas against evildoers perpetuated by people who took the law into their own hands (Gen 4:23-24). Next came the development of the *Lex talionis* in which punishment was meted out in proportion to the nature of the crime ("life for life, eye for eye, tooth for tooth," Exod 21:23-24). A concern to control the viciousness of blood revenge prompted first the concept of sanctuaries and later the idea of cities of refuge. At one time, any shrine where Yahweh was worshiped was considered a sanctuary for persons in trouble (Exod 21:13-14). After the reforms of Josiah and the centralization of worship, though, the cities of refuge became Israel's most important provision for fugitives on the run.

[6]"The Talk of the Town: Notes and Comment," *The New Yorker*, 23 April 1990, 31.

[7]David A. Seamands, *Healing Grace* (Wheaton IL: Victor Books, 1988) 118-20.

[8]Robert Farrar Capon, *Between Noon and Three: A Parable of Romance, Law, and the Outrage of Grace* (San Francisco: Harper & Row, Publishers, 1982) 174.

[9]Frederick Buechner, *Telling the Truth: The Gospel as Tragedy, Comedy & Fairy Tale* (New York: Harper & Row, Publishers, 1977) 70.

[10]Culbert G. Rutenber, *The Price and the Prize: An Interpretation of the Christian Gospel for Young People* (Philadelphia: Judson Press, 1953) 55-74 discusses sin as perversion and lovelessness.

[11]Jean Davjat, *The Theology of Grace,* trans., a nun of Stanbrook Abbey (New York: Hawthorn Publishers, 1959) 10.

[12]C. Ryder Smith, *The Bible Doctrine of Grace* (London: Epworth Press, 1956) 57.

[13]Wayne E. Ward, "Grace," *Mercer Dictionary of the Bible,* ed. Watson E. Mills (Macon GA: Mercer University Press, 1990) 347.

[14]C. L. Mitton, "Grace," *The Interpreter's Dictionary of the Bible,* vol. 2 (Nashville: Abingdon Press, 1962) 466.

[15]William Boggs, *Sin Boldly: But Trust God More Boldly Still* (Nashville: Abingdon Press, 1990) 109, 112.

[16]Reinhold Niebuhr, *Justice and Mercy,* ed. Ursula M. Niebuhr (San Francisco: Harper & Row, Publishers, 1976) 43.

[17]Mitton, "Grace," 468.

[18]David Baily Harned, *Grace and Common Life* (Charlottesville: University Press of Virginia, 1971) 69.

[19]James S. Stewart, *King For Ever* (Nashville: Abingdon, 1975) 155-56.

[20]Frederick Buechner, *The Alphabet of Grace* (New York: Seabury Press, 1977) 11.

[21]Capon, *Between Noon and Three: A Parable of Romance, Law, and the Outrage of Grace,* 73, 149.

[22]Mitton, "Grace," 464.

[23]Smith, *The Bible Doctrine of Grace,* 59.

[24]Paul Scherer, *The Word God Sent* (New York: Harper & Row, Publishers, 1965) 49-53.

[25]Robert Farrar Capon, *The Parables of Judgment* (Grand Rapids, Michigan: William B. Eerdmans Publishing Company, 1989) 150.

[26]*Ibid.,* 131.

[27]David A. Seamands, *Healing Grace,* 66-67.

[28]John Oman, *Grace and Personality* (New York: Association Press, 1961) 176.

[29]James Reid, "The Second Epistle to the Corinthians: Exposition," *The Interpreter's Bible,* vol. 10 (Nashville: Abingdon Press, 1953) 366.

[30]Robert Farrar Capon, *The Parables of Judgment; The Parables of Grace* (Grand Rapids, Michigan: William B. Eerdmans Publishing Company, 1988); and *The Parables of the Kingdom* (Grand Rapids, Michigan: Zondervan Publishing House, 1985).

[31]Robert Farrar Capon, *The Parables of Grace,* 38.

[32]*Ibid.,* 133.

[33]*Ibid.*

[34]Samuel E. Balentine, "Justice/Judgment," *Mercer Dictionary of the Bible,* ed. Watson E. Mills (Macon, GA: Mercer University Press, 1990) 483.

[35]J. W. Bowman, "Eschatology of the NT," *The Interpreter's Dictionary of the Bible,* vol. 2 (Nashville: Abingdon Press, 1962) 139.

[36]C. U. Wolf, "Judge," *The Interpreter's Dictionary of the Bible,* vol. 2 (Nashville: Abingdon Press, 1962) 1013.

[37]J. Arthur Hoyles, *Punishment in the Bible* (London: Epworth Press, 1986) 60.

[38]Daniel Day Williams, *God's Grace and Man's Hope: An Interpretation of the Christian Life in History* (New York: Harper Row, Publishers, 1965) 194.

[39]David Baily Harned, *Grace and Common Life*, 70.

[40]David A. Seamands, *Healing Grace*, 45.

[41]Henri J. M. Nouwen, *The Wounded Healer: Ministry in Contemporary Society* (Garden City, New York: Doubleday & Company, Inc., 1972).

[42]David Buttrick treats this truth superbly in a published sermon. Buttrick says, "Think of a God who doesn't have mercy, but *is* mercy. Think of a God who is willing to give up everything, yes, even to give up being God—there's the laughable man on a lone cross on a hill outside Jerusalem—yes, give up being God to forgive us all!" David G. Buttrick, "A God Who Is Mercy," *Pulpit Digest,* (March, April 1990): 59.

[43]Karl Barth, *The Humanity of God* (Richmond, Virginia: John Knox Press, 1966) 61.

[44]David Baily Harned, *Grace and Common Life,* 70.

[45]Sheldon Vanauken, *A Severe Mercy* (San Francisco: Harper & Row, Publishers, 1977) 85.

[46]Robert Farrar Capon, *Hunting the Divine Fox: An Introduction to the Language of Theology* (Minneapolis, Minnesota: Seabury Press, 1985) 129.

[47]Robert Farrar Capon, *An Offering of Uncles: The Priesthood of Adam and the Shape of the World,* (New York: Crossroad, 1982) 107.

[48]An excellent elaboration of this truth is available in Carlyle Marney, *Priests To Each Other* (Valley Forge: Judson Press, 1974; reprint: Macon GA: Smyth & Helwys, 1991).

[49]Robert Farrar Capon, *Hunting the Divine Fox: An Introduction to the Language of Theology,* 122.

[50]Frederick Buechner, *Telling the Truth: The Gospel as Tragedy, Comedy, and Fairy Tale,* 98.

[51]Dietrich Bonhöffer, *The Cost of Discipleship* (New York: Macmillan Company, 1963) 45-60.

[52]Paul Tillich, *Theology of Peace,* ed. Ronald H. Stone (Louisville: Westminster/John Knox Press, 1990) 122.

[53]Howard Thurman, *With Head and Heart* (New York: Harcourt, Brace, Jovanovich, 1978) 162.

[54]Richard John Neuhaus, *Freedom For Ministry* (San Francisco: Harper & Row, Publishers, 1979) 48.

[55]Robert McAfee Brown, *Is Faith Obsolete?* (Philadelphia: Westminster Press, 1974) 107.